P&O
CRUISES

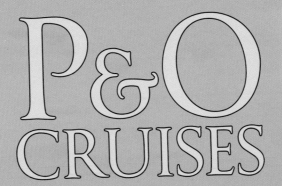

TRACING OUR ROOTS BACK

P&O CRUISES

175

YEARS

A sunset at sea, but not for P&O Cruises as they enter the next twenty-five years towards their bicentenary. (*Graeme Fluellen*)

'You will be more disappointed by the things you didn't do
than by the ones you did do, so cast off the bowlines,
sail away from the safe harbour, catch the trade winds in your sails.
Explore, Dream, Discover.'

Mark Twain

P&O CRUISES

CELEBRATING 175 YEARS OF HERITAGE

P&O CRUISES

175

YEARS

SHARON POOLE & ANDREW SASSOLI-WALKER

AMBERLEY

ACKNOWLEDGEMENTS

We would like to gratefully acknowledge the assistance that we have had from many people in writing this book. In particular, Laura Lake, Michelle Baker and Leanna Rice of P&O Cruises, Campbell McCutcheon of Amberley Publsihing, Michael Penney for permission to quote from his memoir *Sea Officer*, Anthony Robinson for his memoir *Rain Stopped Play*, Wendy Cavaghan for notes written by her husband, the late Mike Cavaghan, Carola Ingall for permission to quote from her book *The P&O Line & Princess Cruises*, Susie Cox and Beth Ellis of the P&O Heritage Collection, retired officers and crew for their vivid and fascinating memories of life at sea, shore-side staff at Carnival House and last but by no means least, the officers and crew of P&O Cruises ships for their patience and assistance on board the fleet during our many visits.

Additionally, thanks are due to Jacqueline Arnold, David Dornom, Glen Gardner, Andrew Harvey, Derek Warmington, Mark Thomas and Michael Whittingham.

Extracts from P&O Company circulars, letters, brochures and other papers in the P&O Archive are reproduced with kind permission of P&O Heritage Collection and P&OSNCo.

Dates in brackets next to the names of ships are those spent in the service of P&O, and sourced from www.poheritage.com and cited here with permission from P&O Heritage.

Cover image: One of the Straths, tendering, c.1935, on a company-issued poster. Reproduced by Kind Permission of P&O Heritage Collection & P&OSNCo. (*J&C McCutcheon collection*)

First published 2011

Amberley Publishing Plc
The Hill, Stroud,
Gloucestershire, GL5 4EP

www.amberleybooks.com

British Library Cataloguing in Publication Data.
A catalogue record for this book is available from the British Library.

ISBN 978 1 4456 0596 1

Typesetting and Origination by Amberley Publishing.
Printed in Great Britain.

CONTENTS

PREFACE

There's no doubt that P&O Cruises holds a unique position in the hearts of British cruisers; a position based on familiarity and trust, as well as the 'P&O-ness' that brings people back to us time and time again. Indeed I can trace my own roots with the company back to 1974, when I travelled on SS *Uganda* as a school girl yet, just last year on *Artemis*, I had the pleasure of meeting a lady whom I recognised from that very cruise. Thirty-eight years on and we are still both connected to this great brand. Of course all the people that have given their thoughts and memories to create this book are part of our P&O Cruises family, and it's wonderful to hear from so many of them spanning the years. I do hope you find as much pleasure in this unique story as I do.

Carol Marlow
Managing Director, P&O Cruises

Carol Marlow, Managing Director of P&O Cruises. (*P&O Cruises*)

FOREWORD

Only a select few British brands can look back with pride at such a rich and vibrant heritage as P&O Cruises. As we trace its roots back over 175 years, it is clear that we owe much of our success to those great pioneers and iconic ships of the past. Without the wealth of knowledge and experience passed down from generation to generation, we would not be the cruise experts that we are today. I find the journey of this company fascinating; from the innovations that have kept it progressive and alive, to those traditions that have remained true to the spirit of cruising for so long.

Now part of the Carnival group of cruise lines, the largest in the world, P&O Cruises, along with sister brand Cunard Line, clearly brings to the group the history and heritage that started passenger shipping, but also leads the growing and evolving British cruise market of today. And with another new P&O Cruises ship planned for 2015, that growth is set to continue. So, today, we hold both the classic and the new in equal esteem, celebrating the past but looking clearly towards the future. And it is with that philosophy that we hope to delight and surprise our passengers, for many years to come.

David Dingle
Chief Executive Officer – Carnival UK
Managing Director – P&O Cruises 2000 – 2007

David Dingle, Chief Executive Officer of Carnival UK and Managing Director of P&O Cruises 2000 – 2007. (*P&O Cruises*)

The distinctive P&O Cruises rising sun logo on *Oriana*, gleaming in the sunshine of Lanzarote, 2007. (*Andrew Sassoli-Walker*)

INTRODUCTION

Mention the word cruise, in Britain at least, and one brand comes to mind above all others – P&O Cruises. Although few perhaps know what the letters stand for, they usually have a good idea of what P&O Cruises represents – tradition, innovation, reliability and service – traits you might expect from a brand with such a long and illustrious history.

It is unlikely that Brodie McGhie Willcox and Arthur Anderson, who established The Peninsular Steam Navigation Company (the Oriental part of the name came later) to operate a weekly mail and cargo route between Britain and the Iberian Peninsular, ever contemplated that one of its descendants might still be operating 175 years later, which speaks volumes for the strength of the foundation they built, with a combination of luck, courage and commercial vision.

Over the years The Peninsular & Oriental Steam Navigation Company has provided a lifeline to families spread all over the globe, by carrying both mail and passengers, while developing the concept of the pleasure cruise along the way. The touch of inspiration came in 1844 when the company offered free passage to the poet and satirist, William Makepeace Thackeray. His published journal encouraged those with the time and money, to try a voyage themselves. It was, after all, the simplest way to reach the Mediterranean, in those days when the Grand Tour was still a popular way of completing the education of upper class young men.

Nowadays, cruising is not just the preserve of the very rich but, despite being more accessible than ever, still holds an air of romance and luxury about it. Many thoughts go through the mind of a passenger as they board a cruise ship but the overriding one is probably anticipation. At that magical moment when the ship slips her lines and edges away from land and the music of the band on the dockside grows fainter, even the most travelled passenger cannot help but feel the excitement of the moment. Indeed, few things in life can compare with a cruise – long sunny days on deck and evenings of glamour, style, fun and entertainment. Sailing into ports such as Venice, surrounded by medieval Italian palaces, or entering the Hudson River with the skyscrapers of Manhattan rising up out of the mist like crystals on a rock; these are images that can only be experienced from a ship; and who would not be moved when standing on deck at dawn gliding silently up a Norwegian fjord, or watching dolphins leap joyfully through the bow wash, while the stress of modern life disappears with the wake. Aircraft may get you there faster, but not with the ease and pleasure of a sea voyage. It is probably one reason why this form of holiday is attracting increasing numbers of people every year. A new port or country every few days without constant packing and unpacking; the luxury of being waited on hand and foot; the wide variety of entertainment and activities; these are all reasons cited for choosing to cruise. For children too – the excitement of making new friends, exploring new places and enjoying all the fun-packed activities on board, certainly ticks the boxes of even the most demanding youngster.

Ask any cruise passenger what it is that keeps them coming back to P&O Cruises and you will get a different answer, but one thing above all –

This page, clockwise from top left: Passengers sip champagne and wave flags as *Oriana* departs Southampton on a short cruise to Rotterdam and Zeebrugge, 17 October 2007. (*Sharon Poole*)

Arcadia berthed at Lisbon with the Monument to the Discoverers on the left, April 2006. (*Andrew Sassoli-Walker*)

Arcadia glimpsed across the rooftops of Venice, one of the world's most enchanting cities into which to sail. (*Barry Simmons*)

Opposite: A few passengers on *Artemis* watch the sunrise in Nordfjord, Norway, August 2007. (*Sharon Poole*)

the feeling of coming home. For a company catering to thousands of passengers a year, on a fleet of seven ships, it is no small achievement to make so many people, of such diverse ages and interests, feel at ease.

Travelling by sea has moved on in 175 years, and while the romantic aspect still holds true – one of the favourite places to propose or honeymoon is on a ship and you can even be married on board – there is much more to do on today's vessels than sit and watch the ocean from a steamer chair. P&O Cruises has responded to contemporary expectations and their ships now offer restaurants created by celebrity chefs, an open-air cinema, spectacular West End style shows and so much more, while still retaining popular traditions such as shuffleboard, quoits and afternoon tea. One thing that founders Willcox and Anderson would still recognise and which identifies a vessel as being a descendant of their line – the P&O house flag with its four quarters of red, yellow, blue and white, inspired by the heraldic colours of Spain and Portugal, the countries first served by the fledgling company.

This is the story of how P&O Cruises can trace its roots back to P&O and the earliest days of steam shipping, to emerge as a highly successful British cruise line.

This page, clockwise from top
Ventura's atrium is illuminated with colour-changing light displays. (*Andrew Sassoli-Walker*)

P&O souvenir bookmark with the familiar house flag inspired by the royal colours of Spain (red and yellow) and Portugal (blue and white). Reproduced by Kind Permission of P&O Heritage Collection & P&OSNCo. (*J&C McCutcheon collection*)

Victoria's last departure from Southampton in 2002 on her farewell cruise, keeping the tradition of flying a paying off pennant from the mast. (*Andrew Sassoli-Walker*)

The intimate surroundings of East restaurant on *Ventura*. (*P&O Cruises*)

Chapter 1

THE SUN NEVER SETS ON A P&O SHIP 1837 – 1939

It was 1837, and the young Victoria had just become Queen following the death of William IV. That year, The Peninsular Steam Navigation Company won an Admiralty contract to carry the Royal Mail between the United Kingdom and Gibraltar via Lisbon and Cadiz.

The story begins much earlier however, with two businessmen, Brodie McGhie Willcox and Arthur Anderson. According to the census, Willcox was born in Belgium of British parents. In 1815, he had opened a small office as a ship broker and commission agent. Anderson had grown up by the sea in the Shetland Islands and, at the age of sixteen, had volunteered in the vavy. On his discharge he met and married Mary Ann Hill and it was her father, a Scarborough ship owner, who introduced him to Willcox. Anderson began working as a clerk for Willcox and in 1822, became a partner. Their first business together was running cargo between Falmouth in Cornwall and the Iberian Peninsular. However, they saw their future in steam rather than sail, and so formed The Peninsular Steam Navigation Company, with financial backing from Captain Richard Bourne, a Dublin ship owner. Initially they chartered, later buying, the wooden paddle-steamer, *William Fawcett.* They soon had sufficient business for a second steamer, *Royal Tar,* these two ships becoming the first of what was eventually to grow into a mighty fleet, known and admired all over the world.

By 1836, Willcox and Anderson had six ships operating a fortnightly passenger and cargo service from London and Falmouth to Oporto, Lisbon, Gibraltar and Malaga. Establishing a reputation for innovative thinking, to save prospective travellers having to visit a vessel in order to see the accommodation, Willcox and Anderson advertised that, 'The Managers have adopted the plan of having at the Chief Office complete models of the whole of the Cabins, by which a Passenger may see at once the size and situation of any cabin or bed-place as well as if he were on board the ship.'

Initially, they ran at a loss, but Willcox and Anderson kept faith in their idea, all the while pushing to obtain an official mail contract. Overseas mail was under Admiralty control and was slow and irregular. In contrast, Willcox and Anderson guaranteed to deliver mail from Falmouth to Lisbon in no more than five days, and at a greatly reduced cost. Despite being repeatedly turned down, they continued to lobby commercial interests. In June 1837, a newspaper reported their steamer *Iberia* sailed from Falmouth and arrived in Oporto just sixty-six hours later. A second steamer, *Braganza,* left Oporto the same day proving that mail could be sent out, replied to and returned in under six days. The Government no longer had a case for refusal. The contract was put out to public tender and on 22 August 1837, they formally signed a contract with The Peninsular Steam Navigation Company (PSNCo.) who were the lowest bidders. This was one of the first private mail contracts in the world. Had it not been a success it is possible that the North Atlantic service may not have been similarly opened to tender and which later put Samuel Cunard on the way to fame and fortune.

Services began on 1 September 1837 with weekly mail sailings from London via Falmouth to Vigo, Oporto, Lisbon, Cadiz and Gibraltar, returning weekly by the same route. For onward travel, Admiralty

The *William Fawcett* (1835-40) was the first ship chartered (and later bought) by The Peninsular Steam Navigation Company. She carried passengers, cargo and mail to Vigo, Lisbon and Cadiz. Built in 1829, at 209grt, she was tiny in comparison with today's cruise liners, smaller even than the car ferries that ply between Southampton and the Isle of Wight. Oil by S.D. Skillet, 1836, © P&O Heritage Collection, reproduced by Kind Permission of P&O Heritage Collection

steam vessels connected with these ships, running alternate weeks from Gibraltar to Malta and from Malta to Corfu and, once a month, from Corfu to Alexandria. Two of the PSNCo. ships operating this service, *Don Juan* (1837) and *Tagus* (1837-64), were advertised as the largest and most powerful ships afloat. Unfortunately, *Don Juan* ran aground just fifteen days after the new service commencing, when she hit rocks in thick fog off Tarifa near Gibraltar. Arthur Anderson was on board at the time and, at some risk to himself, salvaged the mail and cash. No one was injured but the ship was a total loss.

By 1840, PSNCo. had proven the reliability of their operation and so the Governor of India began to press for a similar service to the subcontinent. Willcox and Anderson tendered the lowest bid and, in December 1840, the company was formally incorporated by Royal Charter. With a working capital standing at £1 million (20,000 shares at £50 each), the name of the company was changed to The Peninsular & Oriental Steam Navigation Company, henceforth known all over the world as P&O (and referred to as such from now onwards). For ease of delivery to the ships, the Government chose Southampton as the official mail port and so began P&O's long association with the Hampshire city.

On 27 August 1840, the new 1,787grt steamship *Oriental* sailed into Southampton Water, her arrival announced by the firing of her guns as she dropped anchor. Prior to leaving on the first voyage under the new contract, invited guests were shown over the £60,000 ship. This was later reported in the *Morning Chronicle* whose journalist 'had no hesitation in saying that this is one of the most magnificent steam-vessels that ever left our shore'. On 1 September, *Oriental* left for Alexandria via Gibraltar and Malta. The mail and passengers would then travel overland to Suez and onwards to Calcutta in ships of the East India Company, working in partnership with P&O. *Oriental* arrived at Alexandria fourteen days after leaving Southampton. Meanwhile another new ship, *Great Liverpool* (the first two-funnelled steamship) set off on her first mail contract sailing from Southampton on 1 October and so the two ships began to operate a monthly timetable, leaving on the first day of every month.

Canberra, berthed by the 25 April Bridge at Lisbon, November 1996. Originally named the Salazar Bridge, it was renamed to commemorate the 'Carnation' revolution which returned democracy to Portugal in 1974. Lisbon was one of the first ports served by The Peninsular Steam Navigation Company. (*Andrew Sassoli-Walker*)

Right: In the distance by the headland *Aurora* sails for home, while *Arcadia* moves into her berth at Funchal, Madeira, after lying at anchor, 2008. Willcox and Anderson began calling at Madeira from 1836 when, in spring and autumn, a couple of their ships would continue south from Lisbon for those who wished to spend the winter in warmer climes. Madeira continues to be one of the most popular destinations for P&O Cruises' passengers. (*Bob Walker*)

Left: Poster advertising Peninsular Steam Navigation Company voyages on *Royal Tar*, 1839. Reproduced by Kind Permission of P&OSNCo.

Below: The original P&OSNCo Coat of Arms, with its motto, Who Will Separate Us? (*J&C McCutcheon Collection*)

Opposite, left: Anderson's on *Aurora*, with portrait of one of the founders of the Peninsular Steam Navigation Co., Arthur Anderson. (*Andrew Sassoli-Walker*)

Opposite, right: By August 1842, the new Outer Dock in Southampton (then called the Tidal Dock) was close to completion. The first two vessels to berth were *Tagus* and *Great Liverpool*, both P&O ships. This dock, now Ocean Village Marina, has some steps in the north western corner that are still known as 'The P&O Steps'. (*J&C McCutcheon collection*)

In April 1842, the launch of the 1,800grt *Hindostan* heralded the start of a new extended service from Suez to Calcutta, ending the need to transfer to East India Company ships. Because *Hindostan* was to be based on the Indian Station, she marked a change in design for P&O, being specially constructed for the rigours of travelling in the tropics. Before she set sail on her positioning voyage from Southampton round Cape Horn and up the Red Sea to her new home port of Suez, a reception was held on board, a report of which was published in *The Times* on 14 September 1842, 'The visitors ... then embarked on board a small steamer in the Southampton Docks, and were immediately conveyed to the *Hindostan* ... She is fitted with Captain Smith's safety paddle-box boats, which are so large that the whole of the crew and passengers could be taken in them in any sea ... She is divided by wrought-iron water-tight bulkheads into five compartments, and thus, in the event of a leak being sprung, however extensive, she is perfectly secured from foundering.' The publicity surrounding this ship had been such that her departure was marked with every ship in Southampton dressed overall and sailors manning the yards of the warships as she sailed past. Over the next couple of years, *Hindostan* was joined by *Bentinck* (1843-60) and *Precursor* (1844-69), by which time the Indian mail service was well established.

In 1844, William Thackeray embarked on the *Lady Mary Wood* (1842-58) from Southampton to spend a couple of months sailing around the Mediterranean, compliments of P&O. It was not a cruise in the modern sense, since his journey involved several overnight stays ashore and changes of vessel before his return to London, but the book he published on his return, *From Cornhill to Grand Cairo*, highlighted the pleasure that could be had from sea travel. In it he described life on board, other passengers, going ashore and ports of call. He commented that, 'The sun never sets on a P&O ship', in a twist of the saying that the sun never set on the British Empire. His writings, despite not being universally complimentary, provided free and valuable publicity for P&O. Probably echoing the sentiments of today's cruisers it ended with the words, 'So easy, so charming and I think profitable – it leaves such a store of pleasant recollections for after days.'

In 1845, the company extended services beyond India to Singapore and China, extending them still further from Singapore to Australia seven years later. In 1854, when the powers of the East India Company reverted to the Crown, the company also took over the Bombay to Suez route.

By the mid-nineteenth century most of the new ships built for P&O were powered by screw propellers, instead of paddle-wheels. Tom

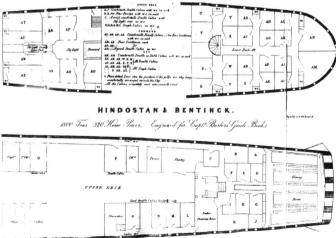

HINDOSTAN & BENTINCK.

1800 Tons 520 Horse Power. Engraved for Capt.ⁿ Barbers Guide Books.

UPPER DECK

Above: Hindostan *(1842-64) leaving Southampton on her maiden voyage, 1842. Until 1884, all steamships carried a full set of masts and auxiliary sails, not only in case of engine failure (which could be frequent), but also to assist the engines when the winds were favourable. © P&O Heritage Collection, reproduced by Kind Permission of P&O Heritage Collection.*

Left: Deck plans of Hindostan *(1842-64) and* Bentinck *(1843-60). The Times of 14 September 1842 reported of* Hindostan, *'... The first object which strikes the observer after ascending the vessel's side is a splendid flush spar deck, which forms a spacious promenade from one end of the vessel to the other; from this deck a handsome staircase leads to the Saloon and to two corridors which extend the whole length of the main deck on each side, and into which the doors of the sleeping cabins open ... By these arrangements passengers ... can pass with perfect comfort under shelter to and from the Saloon without going upon deck or mingling with the crew ... By means of the corridors and the adaptation of the hatchways, a constant circulation of air is kept up in every part of the vessel while in motion...' Reproduced by Kind Permission of P&O Heritage Collection & P&OSNCo. (J&C McCutcheon collection)*

Cringle sailed to Aden in 1858, writing that, 'The *Madras* [1852-74] is an iron-screw steamer of 1,200 tons burden, 280hp and consumes only twenty-three tons of coal daily. I never saw a steamer's furnaces fed so well as this ship's, scarcely a particle of carbon comes down from her funnel ... I had never sailed in a screw-fitted ship before, and had a very poor opinion of the power of the screw as compared with paddles, but this splendid ship never made less than six knots in the worst weather, at a time when I am sure a paddle-steamer would have been walloping in the trough of the sea, shaking her frame to pieces ... and scarce holding her own.'

P&O ships and crew have served in many conflicts in which Britain has been involved. When the war in the Crimea broke out in 1854, some of their largest vessels were requisitioned to carry over 62,000 men and 15,000 horses, as well as dispatches and stores, through the Mediterranean and Black Sea to Balaklava, before evacuating the wounded. Indeed, Florence Nightingale travelled on *Vectis* (1853-65) from Marseilles as far as Constantinople (present-day Istanbul). Another requisitioned ship was *Himalaya*, described at the time as the largest three-masted steamship in the world at 3,438grt. Launched in 1853, she was designed as a paddle-steamer but converted to screw propulsion while still on the stocks. Intended to carry first-class passengers only, she had barely entered service before being converted for trooping, proving so successful in the role she never returned to civilian use.

The loss of these liners, even though temporary, caused major disruption to the mail contracts. Not until the war was over three years later, were normal services resumed, only to be thrown into disarray again when the Indian Mutiny broke out. This time, the 6,000 or so reinforcements had, like all passengers to India, to be disembarked at Alexandria, transported over the desert and embarked onto another ship to continue their journey east.

In the mid-nineteenth century, the logistics of operating a fleet of steamers on long-distance routes were complex and detailed arrangements were required to maintain and provision the ships. Agents had to be appointed and coaling stations set up. Coal was not available in the east and had to be taken out in sailing vessels, carried overland by camel to Suez and onwards to depots at strategic ports. There was no point using steamers since they would use coal as fast as carry it. Suitable fresh provisions could be hard to come by and at Suez there was not even fresh water, except what could be transported from Cairo. Maintenance docks were built at Calcutta and later at Bombay.

The Suez Canal, built between Port Said (a new city built on the soil deposits from the canal project) on the Mediterranean coast and Suez in the Red Sea, opened in 1869 and made a huge difference to the journey eastwards, ending the arduous overland trek through the desert. The official guests for the opening ceremony travelled from Marseilles on the P&O steamer *Delta* (1859-74). Up until 1886, vessels were only allowed to transit in daylight, but when 'traffic jams' of

A print of a steamship arriving at Alexandria, 1842. Passengers would then travel overland to join another ship at Suez to continue their journey east. (*J&C McCutcheon collection*)

Liner transiting the Suez Canal. (J&C McCutcheon collection)

ships began to build up the restriction was lifted, on condition they mounted a powerful searchlight to illuminate both banks to guide them through. The first ship to transit in this fashion was the P&O steamship *Carthage* (1881-1903).

The opening of the Suez Canal nearly bankrupted P&O. It was widely believed by many people that it would not be successful. The Post Office (who had taken back responsibility for overseas mail from the Admiralty in 1860) refused to allow mail to go through the canal, holding that land transport was safer, unless P&O accepted a reduction of subsidy by £30,000 a year, which was not an option. Neither had any P&O vessels been adapted for through traffic to the east. Half the ships were suited to the Mediterranean and half for the tropics; and the offices, stores and coaling stations at Alexandria were all now obsolete. In fairness, the Directors had been looking at modernising the fleet since 1853 but when the Admiralty flatly refused to allow the mail to be carried in iron ships – insisting wooden vessels were safer – the plans stalled. Now the Directors had no option. A few of the ships were sold, a few converted to screw propulsion and the remainder scrapped. Within six years P&O had built up a whole new fleet. The Post Office would not give ground though so, until 1888, the mail was offloaded at Port Said and carted overland to re-join the same ship at Suez, which meanwhile had steamed through the Canal.

Instead of fitting out the new ships with the increasingly lavish interiors that graced many of the North Atlantic liners, P&O designed them to make the journey through the tropics as comfortable as possible, although, through the Red Sea in particular, the entire ship sweltered. Wrap-around promenade decks allowed space to get some exercise whilst offering shade overhead. Cabins were built with two doors – a conventional solid outer door and an inner door with adjustable louvres, like a Venetian blind; with the solid door left ajar and with the porthole opened, it allowed a breeze through the cabin and into the corridor beyond. Canvas awnings were rigged over open decks, cooling not only the deck area but the cabins beneath. Ceiling fans (punkahs) operated by stewards were mounted over the dining table – indeed the deck barbeque originated from these conditions, as a way of escaping the heat of the dining room. Despite these measures, in the Red Sea, the temperature in the cabins could easily reach 100F and many passengers took to sleeping on deck for that part of the journey. Barber's *Overland Guide-Book* of 1845 advised, 'It will be prudent to be provided with a carpet-rug, a pillow and a counterpane or resai (wadded coverlet); for it is very probable that, on getting into a warm latitude, the traveller will prefer sleeping on deck, and the steamer's bedding is not allowed to be carried from its place for such purposes.' Ladies slept on one side of the deck, men on the other.

Between 1840 and 1872 virtually all communication between the UK and India, China, Japan and Australia, was in the hands of P&O

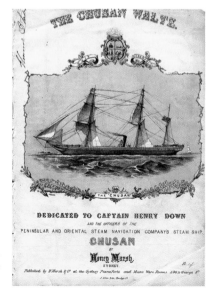

The Chusan Waltz, 'Dedicated to Captain Henry Down and the officers of The Peninsular and Oriental Steam Navigation Company's steam ship *Chusan* by Henry Marsh'. *Chusan* (1852-61) was the first P&O ship to operate the Australian mail service. She arrived in Melbourne and Sydney in 1852 to great celebrations, balls and receptions.

and it is easy to see how they developed an almost mythological status, unique in history.

Kaisar-I-Hind was launched in 1878 and with this ship P&O moved towards greater luxury on board, testing the market for a more refined ship with better facilities, albeit at an increased cost per ticket. Candles finally gave way to oil lamps, there were more bathrooms, cabins had an electric call-bell system and there were refrigerated storerooms on board for perishable food. The ship was an immediate success and it became clear that people were more than ready to pay higher fares for a more comfortable voyage. Further such ships followed, now utilising steel rather than iron – *Clyde* (1881-1901) even had what might be termed an atrium, in that the first-class saloon was built with a mezzanine level which was used as a music room, both areas being lit by overhead skylights. On the next two ships, *Rome* (1881-1912) and

Carthage (1881-1903), intended for the Australian route, the first-class accommodation was moved from aft to midships, with the second-class cabins and saloon over the propeller shafts. These were the first P&O ships to carry a steam launch to tender passengers ashore. Every subsequent ship took another step forward in technology and design; for example *Chusan* (1884-1906) had, not only electric lighting, but also watertight doors that could be closed from the bridge. In 1887, the company introduced what became known as the Jubilee ships – two pairs of sisters – *Britannia* and *Victoria*, *Oceana* and *Arcadia*. The first two were built at Greenock in 1887, the year of both Queen Victoria's and P&O's Golden Jubilee, hence the name. The second pair was built at Harland & Wolff's Belfast yard a year later. The newspapers reported of *Arcadia*, 'Entering a door on the promenade deck we find ourselves at the head of the grand stairway leading down to the spar deck. Before

The first tea ever shipped to Britain from China in a steamship, rather than in the famous sailing clippers, came in a P&O vessel, *Malabar* (1858-60) whose name lives on in this show lounge on *Azura*. (*Andrew Sassoli-Walker*)

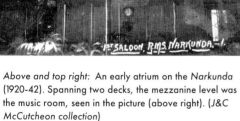

Above and top right: An early atrium on the *Narkunda* (1920-42). Spanning two decks, the mezzanine level was the music room, seen in the picture (above right). (*J&C McCutcheon collection*)

Rght: *Britannia*, one of the four Jubilee ships of 1887-88, the others being *Arcadia, Oceana* and *Victoria*. These marked a large increase in size for P&O ships at just over 6,000grt each. Part of their new design offered improved ventilation and made the vessels extremely popular with passengers. (*J&C McCutcheon collection*)

descending we enter the music or drawing room ... decorated in white and gold ... and having at the centre a grand piano, the case of which is white enamel ... the saloon [first-class] with its two main tables down the centre and smaller tables on the side, seats 138; the chairs swing round in the usual way and have reversible seats, cane or velvet.' On these ships the first-class bathrooms were solid marble and the baths offered hot and cold salt water, spray and showers. American writer, Samuel Clemens, better known as Mark Twain, sailed on *Oceana* in 1895 while on a lecture tour and wrote of the ship, 'This is a noble big ship with spacious promenade decks, a luxury to travel in such.' At the time, P&O was even recognised in the *British Medical Journal* 'for the importance of the step which the company has taken in popularising ocean travel' and its health benefits.

Successive ships followed, each larger, faster and more luxurious than the last. The voyage between London and Bombay now took just over three weeks and Sydney was only forty-four days away from the UK. Some things hadn't changed however and, in those days before

Mediterranean Weather, from P&O Pencillings. In 1891, William Lloyd, sailed to India on one of the P&O Jubilee ships. Throughout his voyage he made a series of sketches and watercolours of life on board, which were published for the Company the following year. In this sketch, awnings shade the deck from the heat. © P&O Heritage Collection, reproduced by Kind Permission of P&O Heritage Collection.

The first-class saloon on *China* (1856-82). The fans or punkahs over the tables, made the intense heat of the tropics more bearable. (J&C McCutcheon collection)

Victoria, one of the four Jubilee Ships of 1887- 88. The message on this postcard, sent on 26 July 1904, reads, 'The above is a drawing of the *Victoria* in which I am travelling. We are due at Port Said this afternoon. Very hot. Sea rough. Love to all from Uncle Alexander. (*J&C McCutcheon collection*)

stabilisers, the Bay of Biscay could still be a trial to be endured. For this reason some passengers preferred to take the P&O train to join the ship in Marseilles. F. Reynolds was on the maiden voyage of *India* (1896-1915), 'Soon the fateful Ushant Point was made, then, oh, the swell! ... This great toe of the Atlantic performed quite up to its reputation, and showed that even a sea giant like the *India* is impotent against its mighty power. How she rolled!'

In 1904, P&O introduced their first cruise ship to the fleet by converting the liner *Rome* (1881-1904) into a 'cruising yacht', renaming her *Vectis* (1904-12). That year she offered ten cruises of between fourteen and twenty-nine days to Norway and Spitsbergen, the Baltic, the Holy Land, the Canaries and the Adriatic. These proved so popular that by 1913 they were using a much larger vessel, the 11,000 ton, twin-screw *Mantua* (1909-35).

The P&O fleet now stood at some seventy ships. By 1881, the home port had reverted from Southampton to London for economic reasons, moving again to Tilbury in 1903. The mail steamers left Tilbury every Friday, sailing alternately to India and Australia. For both routes, the first port was Gibraltar, six days out from Tilbury, where the ship docked for around half a day. Next was Marseilles, then Port Said. At the Egyptian port, all passengers had to disembark while the ship refuelled at the coaling station. Then, through the Suez Canal and Red Sea to Aden – the ships no longer called at Suez. If the ship was on the Australian route, she would meet up there with the steamer to take off the mail and passengers for India, before heading off to Ceylon and Australia, calling at Fremantle, Melbourne, Adelaide and Sydney. The ship would then lay up for two weeks, or sail to New Zealand and back during that time. If the vessel was operating on the Indian Station, it would sail from Aden straight across to Bombay. Passengers for China would disembark at Bombay before joining another ship, sailing by way of Ceylon (to pick up mail from the Australian vessels) to Hong Kong and Shanghai. On the shorter routes P&O operated 'branch-line' or 'feeder' vessels, linking smaller coastal towns with the large ports. Long before cruises as we know them today, people were sailing on these branch-line ships as a way of seeing the world. As G. E. Mitton put it in 1913, 'There are other long-distance passengers who are going across the world merely for the fun of the thing; they possibly have not too much money to spend, and what they have must be hoarded so as to spread over the largest area. They are out for travel, and do not mind how long the voyage is, as it is all part

of the game. They join the boat at Tilbury, and stay on her to the end. They are willing to join in all deck sports, and are sometimes a little exuberant; but their enthusiasm leaves no place for grumbling, and they are as a rule a happy, good-humoured, pleasant set, very sociable with each other.'

When the First World War broke out, P&O ships were requisitioned as troop transports or armed merchant cruisers. Of these, *Kaisar-l-Hind* (1914-38) has to have been one of the luckiest ships afloat. Five times she was targeted by U-boats, the torpedoes missing by a few feet. Part of her 'luck' was reputed to be down to her exceptional speed, as it appears the U-Boat commanders were basing their calculations of bearing and distance on the known top speeds of the rest of the fleet. Even when one finally hit its target in 1918, the ship and all 3,500 crew and troops survived when it failed to explode. The Australian troops on board *Devanha* (1906-28) were not so fortunate as the vessel sailed to Gallipoli. After they disembarked in lifeboats at what is now known as Anzac Cove, the ship moved off to try and divert fire, returning that night to evacuate the first casualties of that disastrous campaign.

By the end of the war P&O had lost a substantial amount of tonnage, yet were still managing to maintain skeleton mail services. They rapidly set about a rebuilding programme, ordering twenty replacement vessels for delivery between 1920 and 1938. Their longer-term aim was not just to recover their pre-war situation but to continue expansion. In 1914, they had acquired British India Steam Navigation Company, a company of similar size to P&O, running complementary services to the East Coast of Africa, among other places. In late 1918, P&O also became the majority shareholder in the Orient Line. This led to an eventual full merger of the passenger side of operations in 1960.

The rebuilding programme fell under the direct supervision of the then P&O Chairman, Lord Inchcape, who took a personal interest in the development of the new ships, including the use of innovative propulsion systems. *Viceroy of India* was one such ship. Launched in 1928, she was the first P&O ship, indeed only the third ship in the world at the time, to have turbo-electric engines. Mail contracts stipulated fast passages of at least seventeen knots – *Viceroy of India* had a top speed of nineteen knots. At nearly 20,000 tons she cost over £1 million. However, it was not her engines or speed that made her so ground-breaking, but the quality and design of the accommodation throughout the whole ship. Every first-class cabin was a single berth,

A William Lloyd drawing from P&O Pencillings, 1892, illustrating the perils of dining on a small steamship in the Bay of Biscay in rough seas. © P&O Heritage Collection, reproduced by Kind Permission of P&O Heritage Collection.

with interconnecting doors. The public rooms were an echo of grand country houses with oak panelling, leaded and stained-glass windows, marble pillars and handmade carpets. She even had a purpose-built indoor swimming pool – the first in the P&O fleet. Usually pools were wood and canvas constructions on deck. These attributes made her ideally suited for cruising as well as line voyages and, from launch, these were a regular feature of her programme. She became one of

P&O's best-loved ships but was torpedoed and sunk by a submarine off the coast of Algeria in 1942 whilst serving as a troopship, with the loss of two officers and two stokers.

In the 1930s, P&O introduced a new series of five liners for the Australian service, known as the *Strath* class. The first two launched were *Strathnaver* and *Strathaird*. At just over 22,000grt, they carried 498 first-class and 670 tourist-class passengers. Introducing the livery well known today,

Opposite: Seagulls rest on the mooring ropes of *Arcadia* with the traditional P&O Cruises' rising sun motif adorning the bow. (*Andrew Sassoli-Walker*)

Right: Richard Parker sailed as an Assistant Purser on *Canberra* on her maiden voyage. He remained in the P&O Group after coming ashore, with his last role in the P&O Group Secretariat at their HQ in Pall Mall, London. Whilst there, he was approached by an Australian whose uncle served in the Australian Flying Corps during the First World War. He was repatriated to Australia from Southampton in the *Kaisar-I-Hind* in May 1919. That year being the 75th anniversary, Richard was keen to mark the occasion, designing and having made a plaque, which is still outside the entrance to Ocean Village in Southampton, formally the Outer Dock, then Princess Alexandra Dock, and home to the first P&O ships that sailed from the port in 1840. It was also the home of P&O Ferries in the 1970s and 1980s. The plaque was unveiled in 1994 at a ceremony which included Australian Military and Air attaches. (*Andrew Sassoli-Walker*)

Below: Kaisar-I-Hind at King George V dock, London, 1933. (*J&C McCutcheon collection*)

Top: Passengers enjoy the swimming pool on *Carthage* (1931-61). (*J&C McCutcheon collection*)

Bottom: *Viceroy of India* (1929-42) was the first P&O ship to be fitted with turbo-electric engines, giving her a top speed of 19 knots. She also had many other trend-setting features, including the first indoor swimming pool on a P&O ship. (*J&C McCutcheon collection*)

their white hulls and buff funnels made them an imposing sight and gained them the nickname the 'White Sisters'. The livery had been used from 1908 for a branch line vessel in the east, but it was the first time it had been used for the large express ships. The bright colour was believed to keep the cabins cooler in hot weather. The company felt that the new scheme implied 'a degree of energy, speed and beauty' and it continues to be used to this day. *Strathnaver* and *Strathaird* were also among the very few P&O vessels to have three funnels (the fore and aft ones were dummies, later removed); the other three ships in the series were single-funnellers. The *Straths* were the first P&O ships to be specifically designed for cruising as well as line voyages. Every cabin had running water (hot and cold in first-class, cold in tourist-class) and the indoor swimming pool on the upper deck had sliding glass screens so it could be opened to the air. There was an Italian-style lounge, Verandah Café and for the first time, two sittings for dinner, which was taken at small tables for four or six people. The third in the series was *Strathmore*, launched in 1935 by the Duchess of York, later Queen Elizabeth, wife of King George VI. She was followed in 1937 by *Stratheden* and in 1938 by the final ship, *Strathallan*, both of which were slightly larger at just under 24,000grt. All five ships were built at the Vickers yard at Barrow-in-Furness, Cumbria and were the final pieces in the jigsaw of post-war regeneration.

In 1937 P&O celebrated their centenary. In London, the Directors held a dinner for selected guests at The Savoy Hotel, where a variety of speakers, including the Chancellor of the Exchequer, Sir John Simon, acknowledged the achievements of the company so far. Perhaps Boyd Cable put it best however in his *Hundred Year History of the P&O*, when he wrote, '1837 – Queen Victoria came to the throne and the beginning of her long and glorious reign; and the P&O launched on its first Hundred Years' History. 1937 – King George VI is crowned; and the P&O sails on its voyage into its second Hundred Years. Surely the omens and auguries are inspiring and auspicious!'

Opposite page, clockwise from left: *Strathnaver* (1931-62) undergoing a refit in dry dock. (*J&C McCutcheon collection*)

A splendid model of the *Strathmore* advertising visits to the ship at the yard, prior to her launch in 1935. (*J&C McCutcheon collection*)

The first-class Verandah Café on *Stratheden* (1937-64). Reproduced by Kind Permission of P&O Heritage Collection & P&OSNCo. (*Sharon Poole collection*)

Strathaird at Port Said, 1950. (The late *Thomas Poole*)

Poster advertising the first two of the five *Strath* ships, *Strathnaver* (1931-62) and *Strathaird* (1932-61). Marketed as the 'White Sisters', they were the first of the large express liners to bear the white hull and buff funnel livery familiar today. Reproduced by Kind Permission of P&O Heritage Collection & P&OSNCo. (*J&C McCutcheon collection*)

Chapter 2

FROM LINERS TO CRUISE SHIPS

On the outbreak of the Second World War in 1939, all P&O passenger vessels were requisitioned. Most had been designed for long passages and had the accommodation, speed and fuel capacity for long periods at sea, making them ideal for conversion to Armed Merchant Cruisers (AMC) or hospital ships. The five *Strath* ships and the *Viceroy of India* were used for trooping duties.

At the company's Annual General Meeting in 1944, P&O officers and crew were cited by the Deputy Chairman, Mr A. O. Lang as having, 'lived up to the highest traditions of the mercantile marine, exposed as they were, at times, to heavy enemy attack, and we were indeed fortunate that our losses of men and ships were not greater. A number of our personnel have received well-deserved decorations for their bravery and devotion to duty ... In one case two cadets ... torpedoed in a fierce gale in the North Atlantic in winter, managed by skilful seamanship to keep a lifeboat afloat for nine days until the survivors ... could be rescued by a Catalina flying-boat. Both lads received the George medal. The second case refers to a junior engineer in charge of a lifeboat from another of our vessels torpedoed in the Atlantic who safely brought nineteen survivors to land after fourteen days adrift in bad weather, for which he was awarded the MBE.'

Mr Lang also mentioned the epic battle of the *Rawalpindi* which, while patrolling Icelandic waters as an AMC two months after war was declared, became trapped between the two most powerful enemy ships at sea – the pocket battleship *Scharnhorst* and the battle cruiser *Gneisenau*. Hopelessly outgunned, after an intense thirteen-minute

battle, *Rawalpindi* was set on fire and sank within five hours with the loss of 264 lives. Just twenty-six survivors were picked up by the *Scharnhorst* with another eleven rescued by fleet sister *Chitral*, which was also patrolling the area. *Chitral* was later adapted to carry small landing craft in place of lifeboats and took part in the invasion of Malaya.

'Operation Torch', part of the campaign to regain control of North Africa, cost the P&O group more than 110,000 tons of shipping (including two of the best liners in the fleet – *Viceroy of India* and the nearly new *Strathallan*). Kenneth Cummings was chief officer on *Viceroy of India*. After being hit by a torpedo at 4.30 p.m. on 11 November, she sank so slowly that he was able to change into his dress uniform before the order to abandon ship was given at 7 a.m. Cummings went on to become one of P&O's longest serving officers, having joined the company in 1918 and retiring as captain of the *Stratheden* (1937-64) in 1960. He died in 2006, aged 106.

At the end of the war, the directors took stock. They accepted that the company would face future competition, not from rival shipping lines, but from the rapidly growing trend for air travel, and services needed to be brought back to normal as soon as possible. However, many of the ships were still under government control to repatriate prisoners-of-war and refugees and move servicemen across the world for peacekeeping and reconstruction work. After the losses of the First World War, P&O had embarked on an extensive new building programme. Now, facing very different economic conditions, they

Above left: Homeward bound, *Himalaya* (1949-74) leaves Port Said in Egypt, 1949. (the late *Thomas Poole*)

Above right: First-class single cabin on *Himalaya* (1949-74). This is an interesting comparison with the current single cabins on *Azura* (see page 98). Reproduced by Kind Permission of P&O Heritage Collection & P&OSNCo. (*Sharon Poole collection*)

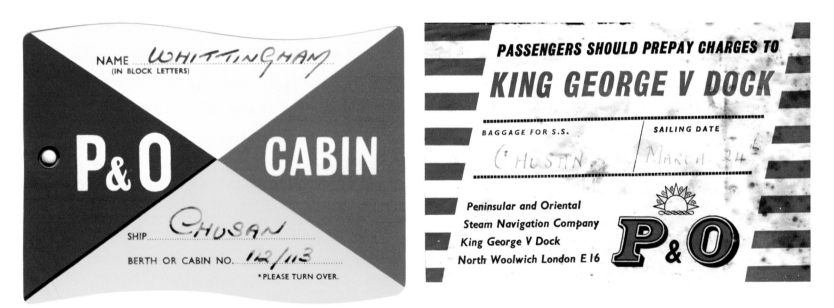

Above, left and right: Two luggage labels for *Chusan* (1950-73). Reproduced by Kind Permission of P&OSNCo. (*Sharon Poole & Michael Whittingham collections*)

Chusan on sea trials, 1950. *Chusan* was the first large passenger ship to be fitted with stabilisers. Michael Penney was Third Officer on her sea trials, 'A good swell was needed to test them [the stabilisers]. It was absolutely calm – not a ripple so it was agreed that the Denny Brown [manufacturers of the stabilisers] engineers would be allowed to take manual control and make the ship roll, which they did very successfully, up to twenty degrees each side, to the amazement of a few yachtsmen who probably decided to be abstemious thereafter!' (*J&C McCutcheon collection*)

ordered just four new ships and set about modernising the others as they were released from government service. The first of the new ships was *Himalaya* (the third ship to bear the name). Launched in 1948, she was nicknamed the 'Glamour Ship' for her reputation for warm but unobtrusive luxury. In service she broke the record by cutting ten days off the run from London to Australia. Captain Baillie commented that, 'the first thing to strike me about *Himalaya* was her size. There was a sports deck as large as a field, a midships lounge filled with acres of sofas, chairs and tables, a vast air-conditioned dining saloon which reminded me irresistibly, in the hush between meals, of a low-ceilinged cathedral ... There were vistas of gleaming alleyways stretching into apparent infinity ...' She was also the first liner to be equipped with a evaporating plant to desalinate sea-water. Soon afterwards *Chusan* (1950-73), again the third ship to be so named, joined the fleet. The intention was for her to operate as a liner between autumn and spring and as a cruise ship in the summer. In 1959, *Chusan* was the first P&O ship to circumnavigate the globe.

There was still a reasonable liner trade to Malaya and Hong Kong and for the time being, the majority of mail was still carried by sea, despite inroads being made by aircraft. The ships were also carrying substantial cargos in addition to passengers. Because the ships ran to such a tight schedule, cargo loading was important to time correctly and woe betide the officer who misjudged it and the vessel ended up as 'short-shipped'.

As the post war years continued, so the map of the British Empire grew smaller. This culminated in 1947 when India gained independence. With it came the inevitable decrease in passengers to that country. However, P&O balanced its trade by increasing the size and number of ships across the cargo divisions. As expected, mail

Top: Brochure for *Iberia*, 1956. Reproduced by Kind Permission of P&O Heritage Collection & P&OSNCo. (*Sharon Poole collection*)

Bottom: The first-class library on *Iberia* (1954-72), illustrating the contemporary style of décor, 1956. At that time most of the floor coverings were wood or linoleum, with few carpets, even in first-class. Reproduced by Kind Permission of P&O Heritage Collection & P&OSNCo. (*Sharon Poole collection*)

contracts rapidly transferred to airlines, but there was a burgeoning emigrant trade. In 1945, the Australian Government set up the assisted passage scheme. Over a million 'Ten Pound Poms', as they were nicknamed (the fare being £10 for adults, children free), took the opportunity to emigrate 'down under' in the years until 1972 when the fare was increased and numbers declined.

In the early 1950s, two new liners, *Arcadia* (1954-79) and *Iberia* (1954-72) were built for the Australian run, with occasional cruising itineraries. At nearly 30,000grt, and with the use now of aluminium for the superstructure, they were taller and wider than any previous vessel. At the same time *Strathaird* and *Strathnaver* were converted into single-class full-time cruise ships. The new ships were a world away from the pre-war liners with their dark interiors and ornamentation. The décor was bright and contemporary with veneered plywood, concealed lighting, bright upholstery and air-conditioning in the public rooms.

Arcadia's maiden voyage to Australia and back was followed by a season of cruises to the Mediterranean and Norway. Michael Penney, by then Second Officer, recalls Commodore Geoffrey Forrest was in command, 'He liked to provide "close-coasting" whenever there was anything to see, provided it did not interfere with the ports programme. This involved me in preparing a complete book of sixteen chapters, with each chapter setting out all the alter course positions, courses and distances, port timings and daylight hours. The initial positions were one mile or more from the shore marks, but if conditions were good on the day he would decide to go closer ... The ship's new radar was of great assistance for providing both bearing and distance off. To sail really close needed other safety precautions. The bridge and engine room teams were beefed up, the main engines slowed to about seventeen knots ... the watertight doors closed, the anchors cleared away and an anchor party closed up. But it was all worth it.' Michael Whittingham provided an example of close-coasting in copies of the daily programme for a cruise on *Chusan* in 1959. Every day there were coastal points of interest listed, 'An hour later we shall pass the island of Ushant which marks the northern end of the Bay of Biscay ... If the visibility is good we shall pass through the narrow channel between Ushant and the mainland, known as the Passage of Fromveur.' Michael Miles also sailed with Commodore Forrest as Assistant Purser and recalls that, 'On the after end of the bridge he carried a small dinghy which he used to sail himself when duties and conditions permitted at various ports.'

The bell from *Arcadia* (1954-79) now mounted in the Spinnaker Bar on board the present *Arcadia*. (*Andrew Sassoli-Walker*)

Left: All about Cruising, written by Sir Alan Herbert in 1959, with traditional paper streamer as thrown on departure. Reproduced by Kind Permission of P&O Heritage Collection & P&OSNCo. (Jacqueline Arnold collection)

Opposite: Orsova (1954-74), photographed from the bridge of an unknown P&O liner. Reproduced by Kind Permission of P&O Heritage Collection & P&OSNCo. (J&C McCutcheon collection)

Cruising was by now an important part of the passenger shipping business and in the late 1950s Sir Alan Herbert wrote a booklet, *All About Cruising* for P&O. Beyond pointing out the obvious attractions – a new port every day or so and pack and unpack once – he adds valuable information about those perennial problems of who and how much to tip and what clothes were required. With regard to evenings he suggests that in a two week cruise, eight or nine nights would be formal, and that 'the old liner rule of no dressing on Sundays or port days seems to break down on cruises, since a touch of evening dress makes people feel on holiday still'. If a keen swimmer he suggests two sets of swimwear but, 'there is a sort of mangle-machine at the pool for squeezing out water and you can leave the suit there to dry if you like'. P&O's cruising fleet then consisted of *Strathmore, Stratheden, Arcadia, Iberia, Chusan* and *Himalaya*, although never all at once. For many people, going abroad was still very much an adventure and cruising offered the easiest and most convenient way to explore foreign countries. Another major advantage over a land-based holiday was with the Government Travel Allowance. This capped money that could be converted to foreign currency at £50 per person per year. Like today, on board expenditure was in sterling, so did not count.

In 1960, P&O's purchase of a majority share in Orient Line brought them a fleet of modern ships of around 28,000grt, among them *Orcades*, *Oronsay* and *Orsova*. The companies had been working in close co-operation for many years and, in 1958, had jointly extended services from Australia to the USA, trading as Orient & Pacific Line. The new combined passenger services would be known as P&O-Orient Lines. With aircraft increasingly taking business from the Australian routes, this was an important diversification for the company. The merger came at a time when both companies already had two larger state-of-the-art ships on order – the 41,900grt *Oriana* (1960-86) for the Orient Line and the 45,250grt *Canberra* (1961-97) for P&O.

Canberra was the largest liner built at Harland & Wolff's Belfast yard since *Titanic*'s sister *Britannic* and would come to represent all that was the best of P&O for many years to come. Her design was revolutionary for the time. The turbo-electric engines were placed far aft in the hull leaving the midships area clear for large public rooms as well as allowing expanses of open deck space. Her speed cut a week off the passage to Australia, bringing it down to twenty-one days. There were other ground-breaking design features that set her apart from her rivals. Like *Arcadia* and *Iberia*, the upper superstructure was of aluminium to save on weight, which allowed an additional 200 cabins to be built. Her lifeboats were positioned lower down and inset above the promenade deck giving her a streamlined appearance. She was also one of the first liners to have an alternating current electrical supply, instead of the direct current common at the time. The innovation was not just in her technology and lines but in the interiors, under design co-ordinator, Sir Hugh Casson.

Canberra, dressed overall in a Mediterranean port. Reproduced by Kind Permission of P&O Heritage Collection & P&OSNCo. (J&C McCutcheon collection)

Right: Inside four-berth cabin on *Canberra*. These cabins could be sold by the berth for solo travellers happy to share. Reproduced by Kind Permission of P&OSNCo. (*Mark Englebretson collection*)

Below: Premier suite on Canberra, 1986. Reproduced by Kind Permission of P&OSNCo. (*Mark Engelbretson collection*)

There were five styles of cabin – single, two-berth, two-bedded, three-berth and four-berth and within each type, up to fourteen different grades. The cheapest cabins were sold by the berth. The most expensive were the four Verandah cabins, situated midships on C deck. Every cabin boasted air conditioning, bedside lights, a radio and wash basins with hot, cold and iced drinking water. Higher grades had a telephone, the remainder had a call-bell for the cabin steward. It was with *Canberra* that P&O began their tradition of commissioning artworks. Sir Colin Anderson, then a director of P&O and an art collector himself, wanted *Canberra* to feature the best of contemporary British art – a trend that continues to this day.

One early visitor to *Canberra* wrote of his first impressions, 'I had been prepared for something out of the ordinary when I had my first look at the new ship, but I must confess to having been impressed beyond my expectations.' He went on to say, 'The most remarkable view is from the bridge, when looking aft one sees an amazing expanse of sundecks below, both first and tourist, with glass screens along the sides. Below the sundeck is the games deck, where right forward under the bridge is the Crow's Nest.' A few regular passengers were heard to exclaim, 'a fine ship, yes, but not really P&O – you should have seen the Jubilee ships, they were really beautiful'. Ironically, this same sentiment was heard on *Oriana* in 1995, when regulars complained, 'It's not like *Canberra*!', so engrained had she become in the P&O collective psyche by that date. James Cusick, at the time of writing, Executive Purser on *Aurora*, recounted that his first posting as Deputy Purser was on board *Canberra*. 'It was amazing to work on board a ship that passengers were so in love with. There were no balconies and everyone met in the public rooms – the ship was always very lively with people socialising.'

Canberra was launched at the Harland & Wolff shipyard in Belfast, by Dame Pattie Menzies, wife of the Australian Prime Minister, on 16 March 1960, with, instead of the traditional Champagne, a huge bottle of Australian wine broken against her bow. Her high speed, combined with the design of the engines being situated right at the stern, caused a problem on sea trials with the bow almost coming clear of the water at full speed. The solution was simple – a few hundred tons of concrete in the forward cargo hold as ballast, although this did nothing for her fuel consumption!

Oriana was launched four months earlier by Princess Alexandra at the Vickers Armstrong yard at Barrow-in-Furness, with not one, but three bottles of wine, one each from Europe, Australia and California, again representing the areas to which she would sail. She was the first British ocean liner with a bulbous bow (a standard feature on all ships today, improving both fuel economy and stability) and the first ocean liner to be fitted with bow thrusters (again a standard feature today).

Oriana was slightly faster than *Canberra*, achieving a top speed of 30.64 knots on sea trials against *Canberra*'s 29.27 knots, and became the fastest non-Atlantic ocean liner ever built. On her maiden voyage however, her speed was much lower. Terry King-Smith was a purser on board. He recalled many cables from head office asking why *Oriana* was travelling so slowly. Then, en-route from Auckland to Fiji, in calm seas, the Captain retracted the stabilisers and the ship leapt forward. It was discovered they had been set at the wrong angle and instead of reducing roll, they were in fact lifting her up in the water and acting as a brake. With suitable adjustment she again matched the speed she exhibited on sea trials. Her high speed also caused problems for the pursers. There were well-established routines to get the required manifests and immigration papers prepared for each port, but these were set around the old passage times. *Oriana* was arriving much sooner, resulting in many late nights to get the paperwork completed in time, until new routines were established. Diana Borcherds was working in the purser's office. She particularly remembers the maiden call at Vancouver, 'Hundreds of schoolchildren were lining the quayside and singing. I was on deck at the time and saw them looking up at the bridge where the captain was standing. They were yelling their heads off at one of our passengers spotted standing next to the commodore. It was Rolf Harris and they all started singing "Tie me Kangaroo Down Sport".'

Quite different ships with the same purpose, *Canberra* and *Oriana* soon settled well into service. With her sleek lines and instantly recognisable silhouette, *Canberra* drew admiring crowds wherever she berthed and became known as the ship that shaped the future. *Oriana* was the last vessel to bear the corn-colour hull of the Orient Line, which was changed to P&O white in 1964.

Meanwhile, their fleet sisters were modernised with air conditioning, stabilisers and improvements to cabins, bringing them closer to the standards of *Canberra* and *Oriana*. The late Mike Cavaghan wrote, 'In 1968 I gained my Master's certificate and joined *Himalaya* (1949-74) as Second Officer. The ship made main line voyages to Australia, taking passengers and immigrants. After calling at Fremantle, Adelaide and Melbourne, there was a three or four day break in Sydney to discharge baggage and cargo and spruce the ship up, after which we cruised

Left: View of the expansive open decks and sports' courts of *Canberra*, seen from the radar mast, 1965. (*Patrick Sutcliffe*)

Above: The Cricketer's Bar on *Canberra*. (*Andrew Sassoli-Walker*)

Below: The designers of *Canberra* came up with an innovative way of introducing daylight into some interior cabins by having a number of 'courts'. Each inside cabin in the court had a corner window (with blind for privacy when required) to allow natural light in from the windows in the hull. Reproduced by Kind Permission of P&OSNCo.

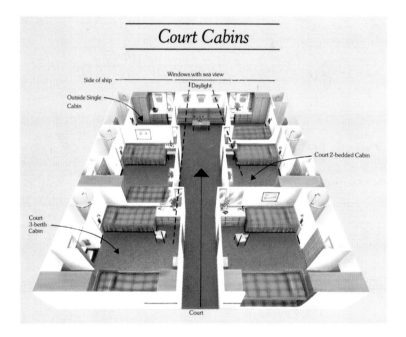

Court Cabins

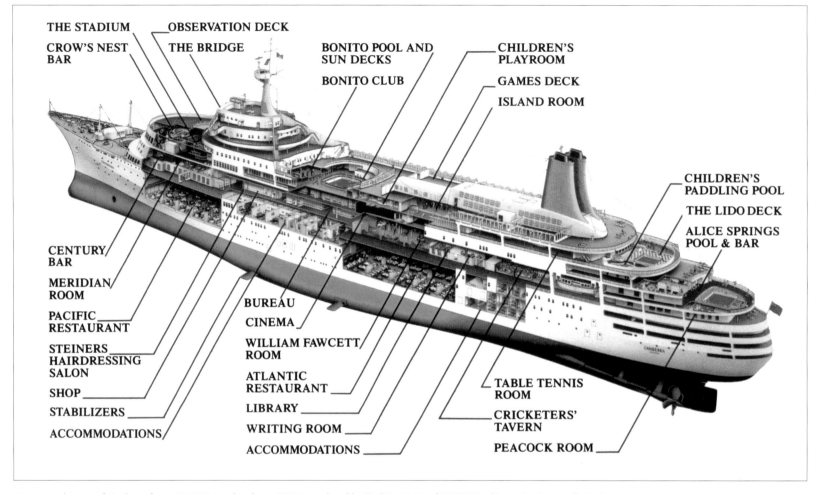

THE STADIUM — OBSERVATION DECK
CROW'S NEST BAR — THE BRIDGE
BONITO POOL AND SUN DECKS
BONITO CLUB
CHILDREN'S PLAYROOM
GAMES DECK
ISLAND ROOM
CHILDREN'S PADDLING POOL
THE LIDO DECK
ALICE SPRINGS POOL & BAR
CENTURY BAR
MERIDIAN ROOM
PACIFIC RESTAURANT
STEINERS HAIRDRESSING SALON
SHOP
STABILIZERS
ACCOMMODATIONS
BUREAU
CINEMA
WILLIAM FAWCETT ROOM
ATLANTIC RESTAURANT
LIBRARY
WRITING ROOM
ACCOMMODATIONS
TABLE TENNIS ROOM
CRICKETERS' TAVERN
PEACOCK ROOM

A cutaway drawing of *Canberra* from a P&O Cruises brochure, 1980. Reproduced by Kind Permission of P&OSNCo. (*Steve Matthews collection*)

around the Pacific Islands for three months, with Sydney as our base port. There was another break to load passengers, cargo and stores for the homeward voyage back to Tilbury. These breaks were magical times, unheard of today, when, in addition to resting the crew and cleaning the ship, there were sports fixtures with local football and cricket teams. At mid-season there was a dress ball with invited guests. They were the last days of an era.'

By the late 1960s, the passenger liner trade had diminished further and most of the company's passenger vessels were almost exclusively cruising. During the 1950s and 1960s, P&O was diversifying into new ventures such as oil tankers, bulk carriers and ferries, etc. As the 1960s drew to a close, there was the biggest transformation in cargo shipping since sail gave way to steam – containerisation. P&O formed a consortium with three other shipping groups, which was named Overseas Container Line (OCL). Initially, OCL operated from Tilbury and Europe to Australia and New Zealand, later introducing routes from Southampton and Northern Europe to the Far East. P&O, through OCL, now had a stake in the terminals at Tilbury and Southampton, paving the way for ports to become a major part of P&O's group activities globally.

Top: The Crow's Nest piano bar, *Canberra*, 1965. This venue, with forward-facing floor-to-ceiling views of the ocean was so popular, the concept was carried forward on *Oriana, Aurora, Arcadia* and *Adonia*. (*Patrick Sutcliffe*)

Bottom: The Crow's Nest piano bar on *Oriana* (1995), offering stunning views of the ocean. (*Andrew Sassoli-Walker*)

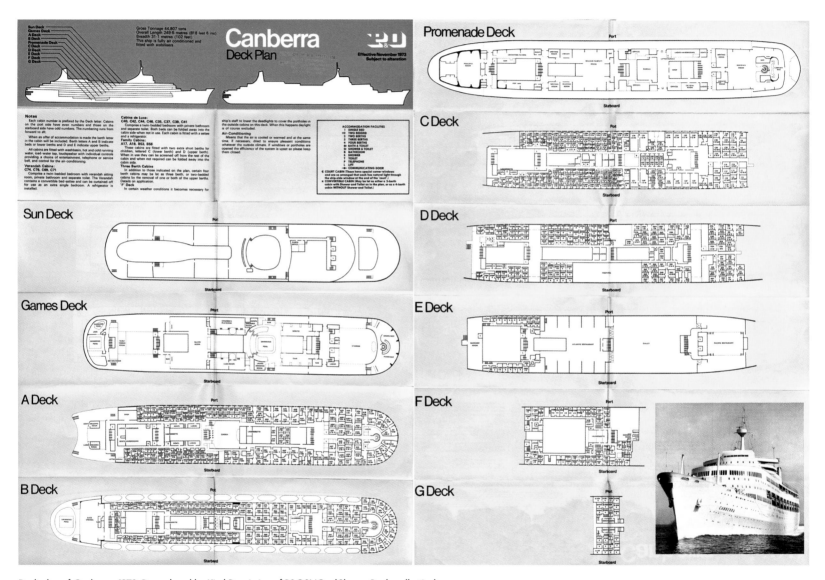

Deck plan of *Canberra*, 1973. Reproduced by Kind Permission of P&OSNCo. (*Sharon Poole collection*)

Oriana (1960-86) in Southampton. She was the last liner built for Orient Line. (*J&C McCutcheon collection*)

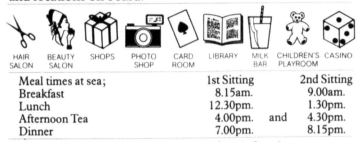

This is not a comprehensive plan of the ship but is intended as a guide to the Decks, main Public Rooms and locations on board.

HAIR SALON	BEAUTY SALON	SHOPS	PHOTO SHOP	CARD ROOM	LIBRARY	MILK BAR	CHILDREN'S PLAYROOM	CASINO

Meal times at sea;	1st Sitting		2nd Sitting
Breakfast	8.15am.		9.00am.
Lunch	12.30pm.		1.30pm.
Afternoon Tea	4.00pm.	and	4.30pm.
Dinner	7.00pm.		8.15pm.

Cabin numbers are prefixed by the appropriate deck and run numerically from Forward to Aft, even nos. Port side, odd nos. Starboard.

50320/880

P&O Cruises
Oriana Pocket Guide

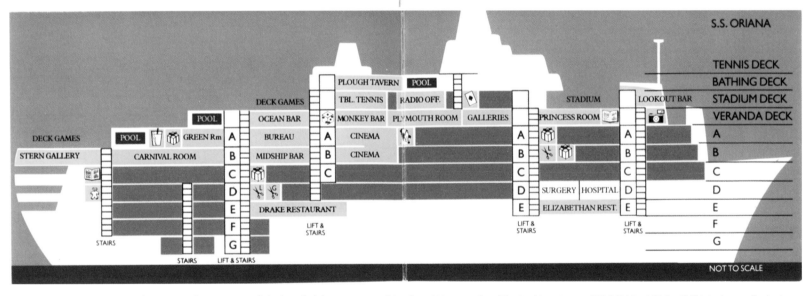

Pocket guide to *Oriana* (1960-74), given to all passengers to help them find their way around the ship, 1972. Reproduced by Kind Permission of P&OSNCo. (*Michael Whittingham collection*)

Two major events proved to be extremely costly to P&O in this period. The first was the National Seaman's strike in 1966, which left passengers and cargo stranded all over the world. Southampton was so full of ships that *Arcadia* had to be moored abeam of *Canberra* as there was no spare berth available. The following year saw the Suez Canal closed to all shipping, remaining so for the next eight years. This was a consequence of the Six Day War with Israel and the subsequent tensions in the Middle East. *Canberra*, which was on her way home from Australia, avoided being trapped by the closure by less than a day, by the captain turning the ship round just before reaching Suez. As it was, she had to sail home via South Africa which required some hasty organisation for re-fuelling, etc. As the Suez Canal remained closed for

Strathmore at Naples, flying her paying-off pennant after a career spanning some twenty-eight years, May 1961. (Patrick Sutcliffe)

the foreseeable future, P&O decided to cease all line voyages to the Far East in 1969 and to India in 1970. This signalled the end of the business that had been at the heart of their trade since 1840.

This could have been the end of passenger operations altogether and indeed that option was considered. Instead P&O chose to expand in the cruise market, particularly in North America. They refitted all the remaining passenger ships as single-class cruise vessels. However, it soon became clear that cruise passengers, particularly American ones, expected better facilities than could be provided on aging liners. By the end of the decade, the *Straths, Arcadia, Chusan, Himalaya* and *Iberia* as well as the ex-Orient Line ships, *Orcades, Orsova* and *Oronsay*, had all been sold or broken up. Modern purpose-built ships were required and the first of these was *Spirit of London*. Originally destined to be Norwegian Cruise Line's *Seaward*, she was acquired in 1972 while still under construction, when NCL pulled out of the deal. In 1974, P&O acquired American cruise line Princess. Established in 1965 by Stanley B. McDonald, Princess Cruises had started with one chartered ship – *Princess Patricia* – the derivation of the name Princess Cruises. When bought by P&O the line was offering cruises to the Mexican Riviera and Alaska – the most popular itineraries in America, with two modern ships – *Pacific Princess* and *Island Princess*. It was the perfect solution to expand P&O's share of the US market. A year later, the television series *The Love Boat*, was first aired. Filmed mainly on board *Pacific Princess*, it brought the glamour and fun of cruising back into the public eye, especially among the younger generation. To cope with increased demand, *Spirit of London* was immediately transferred to the new fleet and renamed *Sun Princess*.

Meanwhile, *Canberra* and *Oriana* were cruising in the UK and Australia respectively. Despite what might seem basic facilities by today's standards, they were still extremely popular ships. 'In the 1970's on *Canberra* we had no private bathroom/facilities and would have to get our steward to reserve us the bathroom down the corridor. If you needed the toilet during the night, it also involved a trek down the passage', said one past passenger, who also recalled that there was a communal room in which to dry your hair.

The decade ended with P&O rebranding the passenger division P&O Cruises.

P&O Canberra is sailing to New York

23 Jan '73 from £39 One Class

Clockwise from left: In 1973 *Canberra* was sent to spend a season cruising in the Caribbean out of New York City. This was not a success and *Canberra* sailed back home to resume her more usual cruising itineraries. Reproduced by Kind Permission of P&OSNCo. (*Mark Thomas collection*)

Island Princess, one of the original 'Love Boats' used in the popular television series, seen here in Southampton during a summer season of European cruises, 1993. (*Andrew Sassoli-Walker*)

Streamers link *Canberra* to the quayside as she leaves Sydney, 2 December 1965. (*Patrick Sutcliffe*)

Cabin steward Stephen Radford on deck as *Canberra* approaches New York with the Statue of Liberty in the background, 1973. (*Stephen Radford*)

A rust streaked *Canberra* in the Falklands. It is still a mystery how a bright white ship, her hull gleaming in the winter sunshine, wasn't hit and easy to understand why ITN war reporter Jeremy Hands nicknamed her the 'Great White Whale'. Another lesser known nickname was 'Super Trooper', after the Abba song *Super Trouper* of 1980. (*Martin Reed*)

Chapter 3

OPERATION CORPORATE & THE FEARLESS FIFTEEN

In the UK, *Canberra* continued cruising as P&O Cruises flagship but this was all about to change. On 1 April 1982, she was close to the end of another successful world cruise. Passengers were enjoying a relaxing day at sea, blissfully unaware of events unfolding in a small group of islands 7,000 miles away in the South Atlantic. That evening, as Argentinian forces closed in on the Falkland Islands, a British Overseas Territory, P&O representatives were meeting with the Ministry of Defence and the Department of Trade to discover if *Canberra* would be required to form part of a taskforce, together with five other ships in the P&O fleet. A couple of days later, as passengers were at dinner or enjoying the evening entertainment, few probably noticed that the ship slowed down off Gibraltar so an advance planning party could board from a launch. Martin Reed, then *Canberra's* Chief Officer, recalls, 'By 0230 on Monday we had worked out the bones of where to put 2,500 troops. We had to keep the passengers unaware of what was happening since the House of Commons had yet to be briefed, so we told them that the planners were in fact Department of Transport inspectors!'

As they began to work out what was needed to convert *Canberra* into a troopship and support vessel, the Order in Council was signed for the Government to officially requisition the liner, along with other ships from various P&O Divisions.

As *Canberra's* World Cruise came to a somewhat unusual conclusion, the company was inundated with people offering help. It was decided that none of the Asian crew would travel with the ship and that most of those scheduled to go on leave would do so as planned. The majority of replacements were recruited through the Merchant Navy pool just for this voyage. Sally Goodman was one of fifteen female staff (soon known as the Fearless Fifteen) who sailed south. Sally recalls 'I was due to join *Canberra* as a Junior Assistant Purser for my first trip in April 1982. When the Falklands situation blew up I was originally told that I would not be joining as I was new to sea. However, the following day I received a telephone call asking whether I would volunteer to go, to which I happily said yes, not thinking we would ever actually get to the Falklands and, like a lot of people at that time, I probably had no idea where they actually were anyway!'

When the ladies volunteered for the voyage, the Navy initially said that they couldn't have female crew going to a war zone, but P&O insisted that they were members of the ship's company and that it was their choice. This was the first time that women sailed as part of a merchant ship's crew to war.

No sooner had the passengers disembarked than workmen arrived to undertake the transformation. The Bonito Pool and forward observation deck were covered in steel to become helicopter landing pads. Rooms were converted into operational offices and most interior floors were covered in plywood to protect them against thousands of army boots. Remarkably, *Canberra* was ready to sail just two days later. The one thing that remained unchanged throughout her military service was her P&O Cruises livery.

The soldiers boarded the following day – nearly 2,000 paratroopers, marines, naval auxiliary staff and helicopter pilots – as Captain Scott-

Masson greeted everyone with his usual welcome aboard post. On the evening of 9 April 1982 – Good Friday – *Canberra* slipped her lines and commenced her long journey south. Every available spot on deck was packed with soldiers, with hundreds of relatives and well-wishers on the dockside waving and cheering. All along the coastline of Southampton Water, thousands watched, sounding car horns or flashing car headlights while *Canberra* responded with blasts from her whistle.

Jan Bacon, now a Restaurant Manager for P&O Cruises, was another of the Fearless Fifteen. Normally a bar stewardess, she was transferred to the accommodation department, servicing the suites allocated to the senior officers of the Marines and Paras. She recalled, 'We often walked in on groups of men scouring maps of the Falklands and planning their campaigns.'

As they reached Ascension Island, blackout conditions were enforced, somewhat of a challenge for a cruise liner normally lit from stem to stern! Every window and porthole had to be covered with anything from cardboard to canvas and many rolls of masking tape. Here they underwent helicopter landing trials so that the wind force over the deck could be assessed.

On 6 May, *Canberra* weighed anchor and set off in convoy while the captain advised everyone that the vessel would now be a front line assault ship although, instead of landing everyone from one ship, it was decided that 1,200 men would be transferred to HMS *Fearless* and HMS *Intrepid* thus diluting the effect of an attack on any one ship. Jan Bacon said, 'This was not what we were expecting as we thought we would be kept at a safe distance and only used as a hospital ship – albeit without a red cross on the side ... We had been evacuated from our cabins below the waterline when the Paras and Marines had cross-decked and so I – and some of my friends – took up residence in one of the suites on my section. There were ten of us in there – safety in numbers!' Eleven days later *Canberra* was deep into the South Atlantic and 'Active Service' was declared, putting the ship under the Naval Discipline Act. It was a tribute to the discipline of the P&O civilian crew aboard that the Act was never invoked.

Sally Goodman again, 'One of my strongest memories is the actual day of the landings. There was an air of trepidation as to what might lie ahead. I wouldn't describe it as frightening; whether that was the ignorance of youth, but I always had a belief that we would come through this experience. However, I do recall packing a few sentimental items in the bag which contained my gas mask, including my address book! One of the other officers had told me he had once worked on a ship which sank and how he had particularly regretted losing his address book. During the evening the ship went to General Emergency Stations and I slept in the back office of the Bureau for the night, along with other duty pursers. I can remember going out onto the promenade deck in the dark and watching the Naval

Opposite left: Workers erect scaffolding to support a helicopter landing pad over *Canberra's* Bonito Pool, 1982. (*John Adamson*)

Opposite right: Keeping look-out on the bridge wing of *Canberra* during her voyage to the South Atlantic, 1982. (*Martin Reed*)

Right: A Royal Navy Sea King helicopter lands on the midships flight deck over the Bonito Pool, 1982 (*John Adamson*)

bombardment on Fanning Head. That was when everything started to feel very real. The morning of 21 May was beautiful and sunny; exactly what we didn't need in view of the air threat. We were very keen to go out and look at the scenery. Because of the strict blackout within the ship, it was the only opportunity for most of the crew to get a glimpse of the Falkland Islands. Once the air attacks started we could only hear them in the Bureau. It must have been terrifying up on the bridge where they could see the impending threats while telling us when to take cover. We hid under the large desk in the Bureau back office. During the afternoon our escort ship HMS *Ardent* was hit and later sank. We took all her survivors on board. This was one of the saddest times, seeing the looks on their faces as they came on board. That evening it was announced that *Canberra* would leave San Carlos water. We could see why the decision had been made, but our thoughts were very much with the forces that had gone ashore. It felt strange leaving them. We had built up friendships and had the greatest respect for them. They were true professionals and we hoped with all our hearts that they would come back safely.'

Jan Bacon also remembers that day. 'We were expected to (sort of) carry on with our work but spent most of the morning at our emergency stations. We were never more than ten feet away from our life jackets. The soldiers who were still on board were using the nearby pantry for tea and seemed pretty relaxed about the whole affair. When we asked them how we would know if the bombs had hit us they just said – believe us – if the ship is hit you will know it. During the afternoon it was suggested that we girls should go up to the Bonito Club to see some of the men that had been injured and transferred over to us. They thought it would help them to see that we were OK so they should be OK ... Soon after that there was another air strike and these poor guys had mattresses flung over them to protect them in their beds. I could not quite work out why I had eight men jump on top of me "to protect me"! When I did struggle to try and get air they told me not to panic and that they would stay there "protecting me" until it was all over!'

That evening, *Canberra* weighed anchor and sailed to an area of relative safety north of the Islands. Meanwhile, in Sydney, Australia, covert plans were being made should it become necessary to also requisition *Oriana*.

A few days later, after another dark day with the loss of *Atlantic Conveyer* a mere sixty nautical miles away from *Canberra*, the ship set off to rendezvous with the Cunard liner *Queen Elizabeth 2*, at the island of South Georgia. *QE2* was spared the voyage to the Falkland Islands as it was felt the potential loss of such a famous ship would be too great a prize for the Argentinians (on *Canberra*'s return, a message was draped over the ship's rail that read '*Canberra* cruises where *QE2* refuses!'). The sight of the two most famous British liners in the inhospitable conditions of Grytviken Harbour was surreal, but gave a welcome sense of home to the injured men about to be transferred and there was much cheering, not only for *Canberra*'s crew, but for the ship herself, which had taken them from near death to warmth and survival. Jan Bacon again, 'I think the most frightening point was when we were informed that we were going back to San Carlos Water to land the Welsh and Scots Guards that we picked up from *QE2*. We never thought we would get away with it this time, especially as the BBC World Service had announced a couple of days previously that *Canberra* was now regarded as expendable.'

However, on Monday 14 June, Argentina surrendered. During the day *Canberra* made a rendezvous with HMS *Hermes* to transfer urgent medical stores for her fleet sister and hospital ship, *Uganda*, nicknamed 'Mother Hen' with her 'chicks' – the small naval survey vessels which operated as ambulance ships. She then returned to San Carlos Water and Port Stanley to embark Argentinian prisoners of war for repatriation. Sally Goodman again, 'The eventual news of the surrender brought with it another challenge for *Canberra*; to return over 4,000 prisoners of war to Argentina. The soldiers seemed relieved to come on board; most of them were poorly-equipped conscripts and they were happy to be warm and well fed on their journey home. Down in the Bureau we were busy typing the handover documents on behalf of the Red Cross – listing name, rank, number and date of birth for every POW. Quite a task on the manual typewriters which we had in those days. We travelled to Puerto Madryn in Argentina where we watched the POWs disembark – there wasn't much of a home-coming for them.' *Canberra* then returned to the Falkland Islands one final time to embark the victorious British troops and in the late afternoon on 25 June, weighed anchor for the journey home to Southampton. As the ship proceeded north, preparations were made for her to be returned to her peacetime role of cruise ship. Once out of range of the Argentinian Air Force, blackout conditions were lifted and everyone relaxed and enjoyed the many parties. At Ascension Island, men from the MOD and P&O joined to assess her condition and how much the refurbishment would cost.

Above: Landing troops in San Carlos Water, 1982. (*John Adamson*)

Below: A homeward-bound *Canberra* at Ascension Island. You can clearly see the forward helicopter deck installed above the Crow's Nest bar. (*Sally Goodman*)

On 11 July, everyone was woken by the voice of purser Lois Wheeler (another of the Fearless Fifteen) with, 'Good Morning Ladies and Gentlemen. It promises to be a fine day with every prospect of a warm welcome when we dock. ... We hope you have enjoyed your cruise and that we might have the pleasure of your company again.' No-one could possibly have prepared those on board *Canberra* for the welcome they were about to receive. Thousands of people lined every vantage point along the Solent and Southampton Water as hundreds of small craft escorted the rust-streaked ship back home and fire tugs sprayed water high into the air in front of the liner. Helicopters flew in VIPs, the last being a Wessex of the Royal Flight, piloted by HRH Prince of Wales. He made sure that he departed before the ship came alongside in order for the crew to enjoy the welcome that was just for them. As *Canberra* approached the docks it was discovered that she had a substantial list to starboard, caused by all the men rushing to one side, looking for their wives and girlfriends on the dockside. The ship would have hit the cranes so orders were given to move back to the port side – or else!

Jan Bacon adds, 'There were rumours circulating that we would first drop off the marines to their home in Plymouth before returning to Southampton. Although we were assured of a huge welcome, our adventure had been an emotional one and we just wanted to leave the ship quietly and go home. As it happened, we sailed directly for Southampton. The crowds at 106 berth were amazing. The families of the marines and P&O crew were on the quayside and the magnetism between the ship and the relatives would have got *Canberra* alongside without any tugs or ropes!'

Canberra finally berthed after a ninety-four day voyage that saw her become a national icon; a proud day for the ship, the crew, the troops, P&O, indeed the whole of the UK. Martin Reed, then Chief Officer of *Canberra*, related a few statistics. 'We had been a troop carrier, helicopter deck, casualty receiving ship, POW camp, water producer and provider of food and comfort wherever we could. We had been alongside but once, in Freetown for eight hours on the way south. We refuelled at sea seven times, the longest refuelling taking ten and a half hours. We produced 39,522 tons of fresh water and served 646,847 meals. We treated 172 casualties and drew 1,310 pints of blood.'

Canberra's engine room staff worked tirelessly under the waterline, even when the ship was at risk from torpedoes and mines. They knew that if the ship had been hit they would not have survived. *Canberra* offered not only practical support, but for the soldiers, emotional reassurance when spotting her familiar silhouette in the bay.

Canberra had earned a place in British history. More importantly for P&O, her well-publicised and triumphant return sparked a renewal of interest in Britain's merchant fleet. After a swift and much-needed refit, *Canberra* was ready to do what she did best – carry carefree holidaymakers over the seas in luxury and style. Sally Goodman again, 'Looking back, it now seems an unreal part of my life. On our return to cruising, I remember our purser, the late Maurice Rudderham, reminding me that it was all going to be rather different having passengers on board, as I was only familiar with "trooping".' Everyone was awarded the South Atlantic Medal and Jan Bacon recalls that hers was kept by her mother until her death as she felt, 'she had gone through a lot more during that time than I did!'

Perhaps the last word should be the farewell message sent to all crew from their Royal Naval boss, 'P&O service as LPH(Landing Platform Helicopters), Fast Troop Carrier, floating Harley Street, maritime Wormwood Scrubs and great survivor of San Carlos Bay was in the true style. Well done. Bon Voyage, Great White Whale.'

Canberra with HMS Andromeda off Port William in Stanley Harbour after the Argentinian surrender. (Martin Reed)

Clockwise, from top left: Equipment being transferred by air to HMS *Intrepid* and HMS *Fearless* in preparation for the landings. (*Sally Goodman*)

Royal Marines celebrating in *Canberra's* Crow's Nest bar the night before arriving home in Southampton. One is holding on to the scaffolding built to support the forward helicopter flight deck above, 10 July 1982. (*Sally Goodman*)

Thousands of people line the waterfront to welcome *Canberra* home to Southampton from her extraordinary voyage to the Falklands, 11 July 1982. (*Mark Engelbretson*)

On the journey home, soldiers relax on *Canberra's* decks, 1982. (*Sally Goodman*)

Above left: Soldiers line the rails to wave to loved ones ashore as *Canberra* returns home to a rapturous welcome, 1982. (*Mark Engelbretson*)

Above right: A dinner was held aboard *Canberra* to mark the fifteenth anniversary of the voyage to the Falklands and her impending retirement. (*Andrew Sassoli-Walker collection*)

Left: Plaque commemorating *Canberra's* service as a troopship and support vessel during the Falklands Conflict of 1982. (*Andrew Sassoli-Walker*)

Chapter 4

FULL AHEAD ON PASSAGE

Cruising operations were soon back to normal following the brief conflict in the South Atlantic. *Oriana* (1960-86) was deployed to Australia and *Sea Princess* (1978-95) was brought to sail alongside *Canberra* in the UK. Gwyn Hughes, later to become Managing Director of the company, joined P&O in 1983, a time when, he commented, 'cruising was not a successful business. However, after much hard work, the team changed the image of cruising, started to generate growth and returns that justified investment.'

Across the Atlantic, Princess was expanding as the American appetite for cruising increased and the company began to plan a new ship for the North American market. Her design was revolutionary at the time and had many new features taken for granted in today's ships, such as televisions in every cabin and computerised accounting systems. Unusually, every cabin had a sea view and many also had private balconies – the first in the P&O fleet. She was named *Royal Princess* by HRH the Princess of Wales in 1984.

The P&O Ferries cross-channel routes remained until rival Townsend Thoresen (European Ferries) bought them in 1985. The exit from ferries was brief however, as P&O bought European Ferries Group less than a year later. By the end of the 1980s, P&O Ferries had routes covering the English Channel, Scottish Islands, Irish and North Seas.

By 1987, P&O was a diverse and vast company involved in everything from shipping, ports and shopping centres to exhibition venues, road haulage and construction. This was their 150th anniversary year,

celebrated with a lavish reception on board *Pacific Princess* alongside the Royal Naval College at Greenwich and attended by HM the Queen. Robin Mason, who now works with P&O Cruises, has reason to remember that year well, 'One of the proudest moments of my life was when I, along with fifteen others from various divisions of P&O as it was then, were chosen to represent the company at the Royal Tournament. We had to report to Earls Court at 9 a.m. on the Monday morning. When we got there the first thing was to learn to march in formation; great fun for a bunch of merchant seamen that had never had to march a day in their lives. We were taken out into the car park, lined up and given instructions on what to do and when to do it. We only had two days to get it right. One of the guys, who has remained a good friend ever since, earned the name Tick Tock. This was a term used in the forces for a person who cannot march. He used to put his left arm forward along with his left leg and so on! Finally the big day came. We had to march out in the finale along with 3,000 other troops from many countries around the world. The atmosphere was fantastic and when we stood there in the spotlight while the story of *Canberra* in the Falklands conflict was told, we all felt really proud of P&O and especially the role the ship had played.'

Canberra hit the headlines again in 1987. The Jones family had taken a year out to circumnavigate the globe in their yacht, a 35-foot ketch called *Dorothy Ann*. They were sailing south down the western coast of Mexico when two large waves struck their boat and she started to sink. The family took to their dinghy with a few flares and basic

Sea Princess and *Royal Princess* together in Southampton. *Sea Princess* alternated between P&O and Princess colours as she moved between the two fleets, which meant repainting her funnel each time – buff for P&O, white with the Seawitch logo for Princess. She returned to the P&O UK fleet permanently in April 1995 and was renamed *Victoria*. (*Andrew Sassoli-Walker*)

design by Italian architect Renzo Piano was inspired by the shape of a dolphin, were called *Crown Princess* and *Regal Princess*. This marked the start of the relationship with Italian shipbuilder Fincantieri that continues to this day.

Canberra was at the forefront of the 50th anniversary commemorations of the Normandy Landings of 1944 when she was chartered by the Royal British Legion to carry nearly 15,000 Allied veterans and their families. A Review of the Fleet took place at Spithead before commemorative services off the Normandy coastline. Some of the ships took their positions the day before the Review, ready to be inspected by HM the Queen on HMY *Britannia* on the Sunday morning. Commodore Ian Gibb was in command of *Canberra*. He remembered, 'It was a blustery day and not the easiest of tasks to anchor the ship in her designated position. We awoke next morning to find ourselves completely surrounded by magnificent ships ranging from Cunard's *Queen Elizabeth 2* to small units of HM Forces. *Britannia* made her passage through the massed fleet and then headed for Normandy followed by *QE2* and *Canberra*. It was my privilege, together with an army padre, to conduct the memorial service on *Canberra*'s open deck, which ended with laying wreaths upon the water. Squadron Leader Andy Tomalin, Officer Commanding, Battle of Britain Memorial Flight,

rations. One of their flares was spotted by the Korean containership *Rainier*, which, although unable to help, sent out a radio message. This was picked up by *Canberra*, which was on a world cruise and only 12 miles away. In extremely challenging conditions (the seas were too high to launch their own rescue boat), Captain David Hannah skilfully positioned the 820-foot ship to the 7-foot dinghy, enabling the family to grab the pilot ladder and climb on board. The family were put ashore at Los Angeles, where P&O arranged a flight home to London. When *Canberra* returned to Southampton the family were there to welcome her and to present the captain with a photograph of *Dorothy-Ann* as a memento.

In 1988, P&O purchased Sitmar Line. Of its three ships, one was positioned in Australia and the others transferred to the Princess fleet. One vessel, *Fairsky*, constructed in 1984, was the last cruise ship built to be powered by steam. She was renamed *Sky Princess*. More importantly, Sitmar had three large ships under construction, all of which went to Princess. *Fairmajesty* (*Star Princess*), being built in France, offered some of the largest cabins afloat. The other two, whose dramatic upper deck

Royal Princess departing Southampton on a summer cruise. The vessel, launched in 1984, was the first ship designed and built for P&O since *Canberra* in 1961. (*Andrew Sassoli-Walker*)

passed overhead in his Lancaster bomber and scored a direct hit upon our decks with one and a half million poppies. We then delivered the veterans to their destination where they proceeded to the ceremonies taking place on the beaches. Quite the most uncomplaining and stalwart passengers I believe who had ever graced the decks and cabins of this wonderful old liner, who herself had done so much for Queen and Country.' Commodore Gibb went on to relate how many of the poppies had been sucked into the air conditioning system and over the next few cruises, were blown out over unsuspecting passengers in their cabins!

Back in the UK, despite her continued popularity, it was recognised that *Canberra* was reaching the end of her working life. In 1988, a provisional decision was made to have a new vessel specifically tailored for UK passengers and operations out of Southampton. Gwyn Hughes, then Managing Director of the company, recalled that, 'P&O investigated a number of possibilities including acquiring a second-hand vessel and taking over one of the older Princess ships. However, it was concluded that a new-build would be most acceptable to passengers and made more economic sense.' When the order was finally placed in 1991, this £200 million gamble proved a turning point in the company's history. The UK cruise market was then largely composed of older ships and having a new vessel would give P&O a valuable edge.

Instrumental in the specification and ordering of the new ship, along with the growth of the P&O group, was Jeffrey Sterling, now Lord Sterling of Plaistow GCVO CBE. As a successful businessman, he had taken over from Lord Inchcape as chairman in 1983 and steered the company into a position of strength. Today, his contribution to the continuing success of P&O Cruises saw him granted the honorary position of Life President.

Top: Medal given to members of staff to commemorate the 150th Anniversary of The Peninsular & Oriental Steam Navigation Company, 1987. (*Sharon Poole collection*)

Right: Cake made on board *Canberra* to mark the 150th Anniversary of P&O, 1987. (*Mark Englebretson*)

Canberra, in the sunset of her career, but still a fine looking vessel, 1997. (Andrew Sassoli-Walker)

Top: On a still morning, *Canberra* arrives home in Southampton at the end of another cruise. (*Andrew Sassoli-Walker*)

Bottom, left and right: A day to remember, *Canberra*, 12 September 1993. As *Canberra* entered the Bay of Biscay on her way to the Mediterranean, the barometer began to fall dramatically and it turned into a day no one on board would forget in a hurry. At 8 a.m. the Captain broadcast a warning to all passengers of a depression approaching. It was a Sunday, and as the congregation at the church service sang the seamen's hymn, *Eternal Father Strong to Save,* passengers began to take to their beds and the decks were closed. Around noon the wind was severe storm force eleven with rapidly rising sea and swell. By 2 p.m. it was Hurricane Force twelve. The Captain hove the ship to, reducing speed to just enough to maintain steerage as *Canberra* pitched in 45-foot swells. As the navigator, Sarah Breton (later P&O Cruises first female captain) wrote, 'Ships were hove to all around the Bay of Biscay. Seeing the gyrations of these other ships, the bridge team were very happy to be on *Canberra*!' At 4 p.m. four life rafts were washed overboard but the wind began to decrease to a 'mere storm force ten' and by 5 p.m. they were able to gradually increase speed and resume their journey to the Mediterranean. They were eight and a half hours behind schedule and lost their call at Lisbon, but *Canberra* made it through with minimal damage considering the strength of the storm. Sarah Breton concluded her account by saying, 'Bad as it was, and having, through fate, been forced to experience the storm, you could not have been in a better ship to do so.' (*Mark Engelbretson*)

Oriana, as she was named, was launched in 1995 to great acclaim. Unlike most of her contemporaries which were designed for Caribbean waters and relatively short itineraries, *Oriana* was built for longer cruises and would sail on a world circumnavigation every year. Her high speed could get UK passengers from Southampton to the sun in a couple of days. The gamble paid off, so much so that, during her launch year, she was the most successful ship in the world financially. In a mark of confidence in their market, and against popular prediction, *Oriana* did not replace *Canberra* but operated alongside her elder sister, at least initially.

As *Oriana* sailed on her maiden voyage, not everyone was celebrating as Jim Philp, now Staff Electro-Technical Officer on *Oriana*, but then Second Electrician for Cunard, explains, 'We all stood on the deck of *QE2* on a bright and sunny day in Southampton to watch *Oriana* sail past on her maiden voyage while below us the passengers waved their flags and cheered the happy occasion. Here was the new pride of the merchant fleet, so naturally this was good cause for celebration – wasn't it? Not on the deck of *QE2*, it wasn't! Southampton harbour shook to the sound of traded whistle blows and with them, the title of Britain's flagship was passed from one vessel to the other. As *Oriana* sailed off into the distance, myself and my fellow officers were left behind in a somewhat sombre mood. It was the end of an era. But now when I look back, who could have guessed then that P&O Cruises and Cunard would now be working alongside each other as part of the most successful cruise company in the UK? – Not me, and I never thought I would ever sail on *Oriana* or any other P&O ship for that matter.'

During the D-Day commemorations in 1994, HMY *Britannia*, with HM The Queen on board, passes *Canberra*, on charter to the Royal British Legion. Commodore Ian Gibb, master of *Canberra*, recalled that an exciting, if unwelcome, incident occurred at change of tide. *QE2*, *Canberra* and an aircraft carrier started their swings, not away from each other but towards each other! Tugs were hastily called to keep the ships apart in the very tight anchorage. (*Andrew Sassoli-Walker*)

By 1997, the fleet consisted of three ships – the aging *Canberra* and *Victoria* (the re-named *Sea Princess*) and the new *Oriana*. This was *Canberra's* final year in service. Her future had been under constant review since 1985. Gwyn Hughes again, 'She was a fuel-thirsty vessel and her operational costs made her difficult to run viably on occasions when fuel prices increased. The plan had been to replace her with *Oriana* but when the time came we realised that demand was such we could operate both vessels in the fleet. However, as the cruising public recognised the high standard of *Oriana*, demand for *Canberra* dropped significantly.' Her farewell world cruise in 1997 followed the traditional route to the Far East and Australia via the Mediterranean and Suez Canal. Her voyage continued across the Pacific and through the Panama Canal before crossing the Atlantic home. She then began her busy Farewell Season.

The affection *Canberra* inspired in the hearts of the British public was evident as she left on her final cruise. Huge crowds gathered in Southampton for her departure on 10 September. At every port the occasion was marked with special events, none more so than at Cannes, where the Golden Cockerel, the symbol given to the fastest P&O ship in the fleet since at least 1908, was handed over to *Oriana* on a glorious autumn evening.

Regular *Canberra* passengers, Mark & Nicola Thomas were typical of those on board the farewell voyage. Mark was introduced to cruising by his parents in the early 1970s with a Shaw Savill Cruise, which his parents saw as a stepping stone to the P&O Cruises holiday to which they aspired. When they were able to realise their dream and embarked on *Canberra* for a cruise to the Canaries, Mark commented that this holiday was so exciting for them, they even fixed the Andrews Shoreside Services' car parking sticker for *Canberra* on the windscreen a week before they left, leaving it on a week after they returned home! On the day, *Canberra* was berthed at the original Ocean Terminal, its Art Deco design adding to the sense of occasion. Mark didn't cruise again until after his marriage,

Oriana, with Commodore Ian Gibb in command, passes *Canberra*, the ship of which he was previously master, 1995. (*Andrew Sassoli-Walker*)

Opposite: Passengers enjoy a day at sea around the Riviera Pool on *Oriana*. (*Gordon Vinnicombe*)

Left: The striking Tiffany-style glass in the spectacular three-deck high atrium of *Oriana*. (*Andrew Sassoli-Walker*)

Top: The magnificent chandeliers in *Oriana*'s Curzon Room. This was originally designed for music recitals, but is now Marco Pierre White's Ocean Grill restaurant. (*Sharon Poole*)

Above: Entrance to Chaplin's cinema on *Oriana*. (*Andrew Sassoli-Walker*)

but from 1989, sailed on *Canberra* many more times with his wife. On the farewell voyage, when they departed Palma, the last foreign port from which the ship sailed, a deck party around the Bonito pool lasted well into the small hours and the exhausted band had to be replaced by recorded music. Despite many subsequent cruises, including the maiden voyages of *Oriana* and *Aurora*, the one they remember best remains *Canberra's* last cruise. Mark went on to add that Captain Rory Smith's aim that it was to be a celebration of the ship's life and not a wake, was carried out right up till 'Finished with engines' was rung on the telegraph.

These pages, clockwise from left: Well-wishers at Calshot wave to passengers on *Oriana* as she sails on a spring cruise, April 2009. (*Andrew Sassoli-Walker*)

Victoria was one of the last P&O ships to be registered in London. (*Andrew Sassoli-Walker*)

Victoria's covered promenade, a legacy of her early days as Swedish America Line's transatlantic liner, *Kungsholm*. (*Andrew Sassoli-Walker*)

A sunny day at sea on *Victoria*, 2002. (*Andrew Sassoli-Walker*)

Left: Saluted by fire tugs, *Canberra* departs on her twenty-night farewell cruise, 10 September 1997. (*Andrew Sassoli-Walker*)

Right: *Canberra* with *Oriana* for the last time at Cannes, 1997. Whilst at anchor, a small ceremony took place as the Golden Cockerel, awarded to the fastest ship in the fleet, was passed from *Canberra* to *Oriana.* (The Ships Photographer)

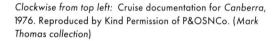

Clockwise from top left: Cruise documentation for *Canberra*, 1976. Reproduced by Kind Permission of P&OSNCo. (*Mark Thomas collection*)

Mark and Nicola Thomas at dinner on Tropical Night, *Canberra*, 1997. (*Mark Thomas*)

As the mist clears, *Canberra* enters Southampton Water for the last time, escorted by HMS *Cornwall* and a flotilla of small craft, 30 September 1997. (*Andrew Sassoli-Walker*)

Below: *Canberra Today*, advertising the farewell Crew Party Night, 1997. Reproduced by Kind Permission of P&OSNCo. (*Mark Thomas collection*)

Right: *Canberra* arrives alongside 106 berth in Southampton for the final time, 30 September 1997. (*Andrew Sassoli-Walker*)

——— The End Of An Era ———
TUESDAY, 30th SEPTEMBER 1997

CANBERRA
Farewell Cruise
10th - 30th September 1997

TODAY

DRESS CODE: Smart Casual

CANBERRA'S CREW PARTY NIGHT

'She has served the company faithfully and impeccably over a long and illustrious career. In her 36 years of service, she has, almost alone, provided the British public with their own brand of cruising.

Her distinguished service has touched the lives of millions, from the Belfast ship builders to the veterans of the D - Day landings - from the emigrants looking forward to a new life in Australia to travellers and families basking for two weeks in the sun.

As the last of the great ocean liners, Canberra's Latin ship's motto, has been appropriately 'Orbem Cingit', 'She Circles the World.' No ship can go on forever and so, today we say not only a last "Farewell" but also a "Thank you" to a legend of a ship, the like of which will never be seen again.

Today we thank all of you, her passengers for sailing in her. We thank many thousands of Ship's Company for serving in her but, most of all, we thank the Great Lady herself. Thank you Canberra, goodbye and God bless you.

(From 'Canberra - The Last Farewell')

THOUGHT FOR THE DAY
Your candle burned out long before your Legend ever did
— Elton John/Bernie Taupin

Her last arrival home mirrored her return from the Falklands. As *Canberra* entered Southampton Water, the mist cleared to reveal a huge flotilla of craft to escort the Great White Whale (as she was still affectionately called) home, while on shore, thousands of people gathered at vantage points along the route. Finally with all lines secured and after a career spanning four decades and almost 5 million miles steamed, *Canberra* completed her service as a P&O ship.

There were a few expressions of interest in purchasing *Canberra* (including one, as Gwyn Hughes remembers, from a certain person called Elvis Presley!), but in the end she sailed to Pakistan to be broken up. The pride of her crew was evident to the last. James Cusick, currently Executive Purser on *Aurora*, was on board, 'We de-stored the ship at Southampton before she sailed off to the breakers. We polished the handrails on the forward first-class staircase every day until we left. We also made up all the beds in the passengers cabins and left the ship as if she was about to embark her passengers.' Gwyn Hughes said Captain Mike Carr, who commanded *Canberra* on her final voyage, later commented it was biggest thrill of his career to set the engines to full steam ahead and aim for Gadani beach. *Canberra* had the last laugh though, as a job that should have taken three months to complete took over a year; such was the quality and strength of the ship.

Chapter 5

P&O CRUISES – A NEW DAWN

When Princess acquired several new-builds from Fincantieri, it was decided to transfer *Star Princess* to the UK fleet and rename her *Arcadia*, the third ship to bear the name. As the world entered a new millennium, a superb new addition joined the P&O Cruises fleet in *Aurora*. Named after the Roman Goddess of the dawn, the Meyer Werft ship took the best of *Oriana*, updated with a dramatic atrium, more balcony cabins and a sliding glass roof or magrodome over the Crystal Pool.

Such was the diversity of the P&O Group that by the 1990s analysts were having a hard time determining the true market value of P&O. The company embarked on a series of disposals on 'non-core' businesses, refocusing the P&O group on ports, logistics, ferries and cruises. A strategic merger of P&O Containers with Royal Nedlloyd created P&O Nedlloyd, at one time the fourth largest container line in the world. P&O Ferries and Stena Line joined forces on the short sea crossings in a merger that lasted for six years before P&O acquired Stena's remaining stake in 2004. In 2005, P&O Nedlloyd was sold to Maersk and in 2006, P&O itself was acquired by DP World under whose ownership the P&O Group of ports, logistics and ferries continue to thrive.

In 2000 the cruise division, known as P&O Princess Cruises was sold by P&O and became P&O Princess Cruises plc, a newly formed, listed company which was independent of the P&O group.

In 2002, Carnival Corporation began the process for a merger with P&O Princess Cruises, which was completed in 2003. The resulting company was called Carnival Corporation & plc. Carnival Cruise Lines was founded in 1972 by Ted Arison, operating with one ship – *Mardi Gras* (1972-93) (ex-*Empress of Canada*) – the first of the 'Fun Ships' that pushed forward the revolution in cruising at that time. It brushed away the old conception that cruising was stuffy, old-fashioned and only for the very wealthy. In 1979, Ted Arison's son, Micky, was named Carnival's President, becoming Chairman and Chief Executive Officer in 1990. Carnival acquired Holland America Line in 1989 and in 1993 the company's name was changed to Carnival Corporation. The company continued its expansion, acquiring such well-known brands as Costa, Seabourn and Cunard. Although a global group, Carnival brands retain their individuality and the character that goes with them. That *Queen Mary 2* was built for Cunard was due to Micky Arison's passion and belief that there was a market for a twenty-first century transatlantic liner, when many people thought *Queen Elizabeth 2* would be the last of her kind.

It seems fitting that with this pedigree, P&O Cruises is one of Carnival's group of leading cruise brands, ensuring the continuation of this famous name and giving the UK management – some of whom have driven the brand forward over many years, such as David Dingle, CBE, now Chief Executive Officer of Carnival UK, who has been involved with the development of P&O Cruises for some thirty-three years – additional resource and inspiration. Indeed, with P&O Cruises now part of a larger group, the ships can be moved between the fleets to facilitate growth where it is needed. For example, in 2005, *Royal Princess*

Three P&O Containers' vessels berthed together for the first time at Southampton Container Terminals during the early 1990s. (*Andrew Sassoli-Walker*)

Left: Micky Arison, Chairman and Chief Executive Officer, Carnival Corporation and plc.

Right: Aurora makes her way down Southampton Water on another cruise to the sun. (*Andrew Sassoli-Walker*)

was moved from Princess Cruises to P&O Cruises. With a small-ship feel similar to the popular *Victoria* (which had been sold in 2002), *Artemis*, as she was renamed, was exclusively for adults. She soon attracted a loyal following, acquiring the nickname 'The little ship with the big heart' from her Executive Purser, Zak Coombs. She left the fleet in 2011, and P&O Cruises has since acquired *Adonia*, another small vessel

P&O Cruises has a diverse range of ships in its fleet. This allows everyone to choose the cruise ship they prefer, whether it is exclusively for adults, family-friendly, classic or contemporary. The vessels range from the intimate 710-passenger *Adonia*, through to the choice offered by 3,100-passenger *Azura* and *Ventura*. All ships have one thing in common, the same renowned P&O Cruises atmosphere, style of service and commitment to their passengers.

The fleet continues to sail to the popular cruising destinations of the Western and Eastern Mediterranean, Baltic, Scandinavia, USA, Canada and the Caribbean with a choice of world cruises during the winter months as well as fly-cruises to various sunny destinations.

Left: The Crystal Pool and distinctive funnel of *Artemis*, pictured in Piraeus, the port for Athens, 3 May 2010. This was *Artemis'* final season with P&O Cruises. (*Sharon Poole*)

Above: *Artemis* on a snowy day at Copenhagen, December 2010. (*Sharon Poole*)

Opposite: The beautiful profile of *Aurora* has become a modern-day classic. (*Andrew Sassoli-Walker*)

Oriana 1995

Godmother: Queen Elizabeth II

Now the oldest ship in the fleet, *Oriana* attracts those who like traditional-style cruising. Affectionately known by those who work in the fleet as *The Big* O (as was her previous namesake), she is the reference ship; the one built to appeal to existing as well as future passengers (as understood in 1995) and the one that future ships had to match, or beat. Such was the importance of her arrival into the UK cruise market, that she was named by HM the Queen in a lavish ceremony the like of which had not been seen in many years. As Commodore Ian Gibb, *Oriana's* first Master, said, 'She was a leap of faith by P&O. Canberra had, almost single-handedly, carried the banner of the British cruise industry for a number of years, but even her most dedicated supporters realised that her days were numbered. *Oriana* was to become the worthy successor of a grand tradition of cruising by P&O. Incorporated into her design were many of the features for which P&O were noted including a variety of public rooms, both intimate and large, a well-stocked library plus many innovative features deemed necessary to entice a new generation of British passengers. Without *Oriana*, and her dedicated and friendly ships' company, as a template for the future, there would not now be seven P&O Cruises' passenger ships, plying the oceans today.'

She was built in the Papenburg shipyards of Meyer Werft in Germany and, at the time, was undeniably the ship to which all others would aspire, incorporating everything P&O knew their clientele loved or desired – a modern cruise ship finally designed for Britain. The then chairman, Lord Sterling, aware he would have to win over stalwart *Canberra* fans, specified a traditional appearance for *Oriana* – with long bow, streamlined hull, a large buff-coloured funnel and elegant tiered stern decks. At her latest major refit in November 2011, she was converted into a ship exclusively for adults, her appeal resting in her timeless classic interiors and spacious teak decks.

Top: Oriana lies overnight at Southampton with *Canberra* berthed to the left, 1995. (*Andrew Sassoli-Walker*)

Middle: A flotilla of small craft escort *Oriana* on her maiden voyage, April 1995. (*Andrew Sassoli-Walker*)

Bottom: Executive Purser James Cusick (left) and Captain David Pembridge on the bridge of *Aurora*. Yes – that is a monkey hiding behind the ships bell! (*Andrew Sassoli-Walker*)

Above left: The Thackeray Room on *Oriana*, with furniture designed by the Queen's nephew David Linley. (*Andrew Sassoli-Walker*)

Above right: The Theatre Royal on Oriana. This venue, with its uninterrupted sight lines, and air conditioning built into every seat, was amazing for passengers used to *Canberra's* hot and stuffy Stadium Theatre. (*Andrew Sassoli-Walker*)

Mark and Nicola Thomas were on her maiden voyage, 'In the early 1990s there was no access to online news and websites so *Oriana's* entry into service received huge newspaper, radio and television coverage, even an *Oriana* supplement in *The Times*. We had looked forward to the maiden voyage for years but despite reading all we could, nothing prepared us for our first impressions on boarding. We had been transported from that world of P&O ships we knew so well from *Canberra*, to a fresh new ship with the latest facilities but which somehow managed to retain tradition in her décor and an ocean liner pedigree in her design. A ship designed for fast, deep-ocean cruising with stores and self-sufficiency for long passages but also breaking new ground and with acres of the outside deck space so appreciated by British passengers. We take so much for granted in terms of facilities on modern ships and they continue to evolve with every new-build. Back in 1995 *Oriana* was not so much evolutionary as revolutionary; she was such a step-change in all respects. *Oriana* paved the way for the cruising product we enjoy today and as such deserves recognition as another P&O ship that shaped the future.'

James Cusick was purser on board. He recalls, 'So many new computerised systems for all of us to get used to – I had never used email before – I soon learned to type! It was so exciting to have such streamlined galleys and pantries and cabins with balconies. Until *Oriana* I only knew *Canberra* and the two ships were like day and night. You always wonder what might go wrong on a maiden voyage but I have to say it was a very smooth operation. Everywhere we went we got a special welcome ceremony on the dock with officials coming on board at each port to present the captain with a plaque to commemorate the occasion. With her classic interior and quality build *Oriana* was destined to become a firm favourite and still is today.'

Aurora 2000

Godmother: HRH The Princess Royal

Following the success of *Oriana*, P&O Princess went back to Meyer Werft for another ship, to be introduced at the start of the new millennium. A sister ship, but not a twin, *Aurora* featured more balcony cabins – her clever design ensuring she could still fit through the Panama Canal by making her wider above the level of the promenade deck. Current Executive Purser James Cusick worked for a year on the project team prior to her launch. 'This gave me a great insight into the shore-side operation and systems – I have the greatest admiration for my shore-based colleagues, but I much prefer the buzz of working at sea! *Aurora* was named by HRH The Princess Royal. That was a day and night I will never forget – my guest list for the top suites and mini suites read like a "Who's Who".'

Aurora did not have the most auspicious start to her career, suffering an overheated propeller bearing that curtailed her maiden voyage, but what could have been a public relations disaster was turned around by the impeccable way the incident was handled. The ship soon settled into service and is still extremely popular. The interior is as contemporary as *Oriana* is classic, her most notable feature being the stunning Laliqué-style waterfall spanning the four-deck atrium. She was also the first P&O Cruises ship to have a sliding glass roof, or magrodome, over the central pool.

Karen McCleod, an employee of Carnival UK since 2003, has a very special reason to remember *Aurora*. 'My first cruise was a two-week voyage to Norway in July 2004. While on the top deck, at anchor off Spitsbergen, my boyfriend of five years, Ian, proposed to me! The landscape was breath-taking, we'd had an great time ashore and, even though the wind chill factor was about -3C, the whole experience was amazing (although I must have looked very unattractive with my fleece pulled up round my ears and sleeves pulled down over my hands to try to keep warm!). We celebrated with a sail-away drink of mulled wine – then at dinner that evening ordered a bottle of champagne to share the good news with our dining companions. We got married in April 2006 and our honeymoon was spent on *Oriana* from Southampton to the Caribbean and back.'

Left: Aurora in the spectacular harbour at Sydney on her annual world cruise. (P&O Cruises)

Opposite: Aurora entering the locks of the Panama Canal. Although larger than *Oriana*, her clever design ensured she could still fit through the Panama Canal locks by making her wider above the level of the promenade deck. (P&O Cruises)

Clockwise from left: Rainbows form through the water from the fire tugs as they escort *Aurora* on her maiden voyage, May Bank Holiday, 2000. (*Andrew Sassoli-Walker*)

The striking Laliqué-style waterfall in the four-deck atrium of *Aurora*. (*Andrew Sassoli-Walker*)

Aurora backed by the snow-covered peaks of Spitsbergen, one of the most northerly destinations the fleet visits. (P&O Cruises)

Oceana 2002

Godmother: HRH The Princess Royal

Oceana, with her sleek lines and stunning atrium, is a glamorous ship. At 77,000grt she is a mid-sized ship with a capacity of around 2,000 passengers. She was built in the Fincantieri shipyard in Monfalcone, Italy, as *Ocean Princess* for the Princess division of P&O. For this reason her interior design is slightly different from ships designed for the UK. Whereas *Oriana* and *Aurora* have rooms off a main corridor, most of the lounges and bars are walk-through on *Oceana*, making it a great ship for people-watching. At the stern, one of the pools is part-covered by a glass roof, offering some shelter. With a wide range of bars and lounges, four pools and the option of Freedom Dining as well as the more traditional fixed seating, she is ideal for new-comers to cruising.

A touch of Mediterranean flair comes in the form of Captain Angelo Vago, the first Italian captain in the P&O Cruises fleet. He writes, 'Not everyone knows that every time *Oceana* sails from Southampton, to "officially start the cruise" two large trays of food are delivered to the bridge from the galley at 6 p.m. sharp or, as we say on the bridge, at 1800 sharp! At this time, many off-duty deck officers return to the bridge along with, increasingly often, some engineers and hotel officers too – an interdepartmental gathering you might say! Believe me, the sandwiches are just fabulous. A ciabatta is split as a sandwich, a generous slice of ham over a layer of sliced tomato and

Left: Oceana at the Queen Elizabeth II Terminal in Southampton, as the Battle of Britain Memorial Flight soars overhead during a commemorative display over the city in 2010. (*Andrew Sassoli-Walker*)

Above: The unusual semi-covered Terrace Bar and Pool at the stern of *Oceana*. (*Andrew Sassoli-Walker*)

Left: Passengers enjoy a sunny afternoon on deck on *Oceana* at Lisbon, 18 April 2007. (*Sharon Poole*)

Opposite, clockwise from top left: The glittering atrium on *Oceana*. (*Andrew Sassoli-Walker*)

The attractive water feature in the atrium on *Oceana*, 2011. (*Sharon Poole*)

Helen Skoins, Executive Purser on *Oceana*, 2011. (*Andrew Sassoli-Walker*)

a slice of cheese too. Put the sandwich in the oven for several minutes until the cheese is melted, the ham starts to become crispy and the tomato is melting – so delicious! All the Southampton pilots love these sandwiches, patented *Oceana*. It's now a tradition that several of these ciabattas (leftover from the expanded waists of the bridge team) are lovingly wrapped in aluminium and delivered to the pilot boat crew. So next time when you see the pilot disembark *Oceana*, note the new garbage bag leaving the ship before the pilot! Everyone wants to pilot *Oceana* and who can blame them? A big thank you to the Chef and to his team.'

Helen Skoins is Executive Purser. She has been working for P&O Cruises since 1996 and has served on almost all the ships in the fleet. She loves the variety of the job, 'Life at sea is always exciting. Part of this comes from the waking up each morning and being in a new country, you never

know what the day may bring!' From meeting port agents and local officials to dispatching passengers on tours, there are many aspects to the job. She continues, 'I have to sit in on different meetings, or do rounds of the ship with the captain to ensure everything is as it should be. I spend most of my day out and about, catching up with passengers and crew on how their day has gone, what plans they have for the rest of the cruise while ensuring that we are delivering the highest level of service to all on board. As soon as we are ready to leave port, I visit the bridge to "sign off", confirming that, from a hotel perspective, the ship is ready to sail and all passengers and crew are accounted for. This means I get to see every departure from the bridge which is a great privilege. Then it's off to get changed into my evening uniform and again around the ship, checking on the entertainment, dinner, etc.'

Arcadia 2005

Godmother: Dame Kelly Holmes

Arcadia was the first new P&O Cruises ship for five years, the first to be directly built for the brand by Fincantieri, at their yard in Marghera and the first ship in the fleet exclusively for adults. Such was the interest in her arrival, advance bookings for her whole maiden season ensured she was almost sold out even before she was launched.

Arcadia arrived for the first time in atrocious weather with gale force conditions and heavy rain, but the sight of her gleaming white hull, fluttering house flag and dressed overall, added a splash of colour to her home port of Southampton that day.

Karen Matthews and her husband Kevin needed a break and relaxation in a year in which Karen had suffered major health problems. Kevin writes, 'For first-time cruisers looking for something special to celebrate a fiftieth birthday, this particular itinerary and this particular ship were the perfect choices to catch the cruising bug. The seven-day cruise aboard *Arcadia* was just what the doctor ordered in more ways than one. Exploring the delights on every deck was made all the more enjoyable by the friendliness and dedication of the crew for whom nothing was too much trouble. Our destination – the Norwegian Fjords – with its stunning landscape and pure clean air was an added bonus. Our highlights – dressing up for dinner and not being laughed at (we come from Bridgwater in Somerset!) and going to the theatre and having a late night drink while not having to get a taxi home. Our only disappointment – not seeing a whale in the North Sea!'

Heather and Malcolm Dove got married on *Arcadia* in 2008. 'When my partner proposed to me on 1 December 2007 we decided that as cruising addicts, it would be fantastic to celebrate our wedding on *Arcadia* at Christmas 2008. We had first sailed on the ship in 2006 and loved her. Although we both have friends and families, as senior citizens we thought that if we had a large party to celebrate when we got back no-one would mind so I contacted the Wedding Planning Department of P&O Cruises. There were people on board we knew through online cruise forums such as P&O's Cruise Connections, so we invited them to be our witnesses and best man. When we boarded *Arcadia* we were ushered through the Priority Boarding check-in, together with my wedding dress, bouquets and buttonholes, and escorted to our balcony cabin. On arrival there we found a lovely bottle

Above: Dressed overall for her maiden arrival at Southampton, *Arcadia* gives some colour to a stormy day in April 2005. (*Andrew Sassoli-Walker*)

Below: With the traditional fire tug salute, *Arcadia* leaves on her maiden voyage – a sixteen-night cruise to the Western Mediterranean, 14 April 2005. (*Andrew Sassoli-Walker*)

of champagne, glasses, chocolates, a flower arrangement and an invitation card to meet our on board wedding co-ordinator, Daniel. I can honestly say we had the most brilliant time. The actual ceremony took place at 5 p.m. on Christmas Day and was conducted by Captain Ian Walters. We were told that the ship had to be at least twelve miles out in international waters for the ceremony to be legal and you could see in the wake of the ship where she had changed course specially. I loved getting married on board ship; we had a wonderful time.'

Word of mouth is often the best recommendation, so after being told many times how good cruising was by their niece, Raffaella and Barry Simmons thought that they would first visit *Arcadia*. Their tour, followed by a three course lunch, dispelled any myths they had heard about cruising. The next day they took the plunge, with a sixteen-night Mediterranean cruise. On board, their expectations were exceeded. Among several wonderful destinations the highlight for them was Venice. Many passengers were on deck early, peering through the morning mist for the first glimpse of the famous landmarks, explained with a broadcast commentary. The reassurance of organised trips meant that the whole holiday was stress free. Their Ruby Wedding Anniversary was in 2011 and they chose to celebrate it as sea, this time on *Ventura*.

Clockwise from top left: During *Arcadia's* refit in 2009, a new stern section was fitted, giving her thirty-four additional cabins and more space on the Aquarius Deck. (P&O Cruises)

The Rising Sun pub on *Arcadia*, decorated for Christmas, 2009. (*Sharon Poole*)

The boutique cinema, *Arcadia*, August 2011. In 2009 *Arcadia* underwent a refit. Part of this was to convert the cyber-study into a thirty-seat cinema, something the ship had lacked before. (*Sharon Poole*)

Above left: The sun rising over the Tagus River as *Arcadia* arrives in Lisbon, April 1996. The magrodome over the pool is open. (*Andrew Sassoli-Walker*)

Above right: Heather & Malcolm Dove just after their wedding, performed on board *Arcadia* by Captain Ian Walters, Christmas Day 2008. (*Heather Dove*)

Below left: Passengers can enjoy swimming in all weathers with the retractable glazed roof or magrodome over the Neptune Pool on *Arcadia*. (*Andrew Sassoli-Walker*)

Below right: Karen and Kevin Matthews beside the Aquarius Pool on *Arcadia*, on their first cruise, 2010. (*Karen Matthews*)

Ventura 2008

Godmother: Dame Helen Mirren

Ventura is one of the two largest vessels in the P&O Cruises fleet and, at the time of her launch, was the largest cruise ship ever built for the UK market at 115,000grt. Her fifteen decks are packed with family-friendly facilities, including eight restaurants, six shops, five pools and three show lounges, one of which is the Arena – the largest theatre on a British cruise ship. Other signature features include the Metropolis Bar, set right at the top of the ship with stunning views both fore and aft and with a 20-metre plasma video wall with real-time moving images of famous cities around the world.

Ventura was built at Fincantieri's Monfalcone shipyard in Italy. In June 2007, her temporary Godmother or Madrina, watched as a newly-minted £2 coin and Euro were welded to the foot of the mast in the traditional ceremony to bring good luck to a ship. Then the dock was flooded and Ventura floated out into the Italian sunshine. This was a far cry from her arrival in Southampton nine months later during an unseasonable blizzard. Even with the unusual weather, crowds were out to greet her as *Aurora* saluted her new sister with blasts of her whistle.

On 18 April 2008, *Ventura* left on her maiden voyage, a seventeen-night cruise to the Mediterranean. Captain Alistair Clark, *Ventura*'s first and, at the time of writing, current master, commented that she is his favourite ship among those he has commanded and that it was an honour to be selected as the first captain.

Angie Hampton had never considered a cruise due to her fear of water, but her husband, Steve, had grown up watching *Canberra* sail in and out of Southampton. Some friends convinced them to try a party cruise on *Aurora* and having enjoyed themselves, they booked a Caribbean fly cruise. With three children, they wanted a family-friendly ship and *Ventura* fitted the bill perfectly. Steve and Angie took off from a sub-zero UK with their children, Daniel aged thirteen, Joshua aged nine and Abigail aged six. As soon as they landed in Barbados they boarded buses to the ship, everyone craning their necks to be the first to sight *Ventura*. Once they had found their cabin and been greeted by their steward, the holiday had begun. The children fell into different age groups and therefore different on board clubs. Abigail was in the Surfers Club and one of the activities was making dinner for all the parents. She became a waitress for everyone, complete with uniform, taking orders then finally serving the diners. Joshua was in the Scuba Club and they took part in a treasure hunt around the ship. They also made cushions from recyclable materials, the challenge being that an egg dropped onto the cushion must not break. Joshua was very proud that his egg remained intact. Asked his opinion of *Ventura*, only one word sprang to mind – awesome! Daniel, the eldest, attended the H2O club, where he also enjoyed the computer games along with various new card games, which he played for the first time. One of his highlights was the chance to be a DJ, selecting the playlist for the club and taking part in the Rock School playing the drums to Michael Jackson's *Beat It* in front of 200 people in the Havana Club, to a huge round of applause at the end.

Ventura creates a foaming wake through the blue Mediterranean. (Barry Simmons)

Clockwise from top left: The view forward from outside the Metropolis Bar on *Ventura*. (*Barry Simmons*)

Metropolis Bar, *Ventura*. A 20-metre plasma screen brings to life a different city skyline each evening, including London, New York, Hong Kong, Shanghai and Sydney. (P&O Cruises)

On a still summer morning, two swans feed, blissfully unaware of *Ventura*'s arrival at Southampton after another successful cruise. (*Andrew Sassoli-Walker*)

Opposite, clockwise from top left: *Ventura* was met by a blizzard on her maiden arrival at Southampton in April 2008, that just cleared as she sailed into port escorted by the customary fire tug. (*Andrew Sassoli-Walker*)

Ventura basks in the sunshine while at anchor off Monaco. (*Barry Simmons*)

Many of *Ventura*'s interior fittings were designed by Nick Munro who delighted in using nautical references in a surprising and unique way. For example, this cabin hospitality tray is based on the shape of the funnels of the old liners. (P&O Cruises)

Next page, clockwise from top left: Captain Alistair Clark, master of *Ventura*. (*Andrew Sassoli-Walker*)

Abigail Hampton's teddy, 'Lego Bear', enjoyed his cruise on *Ventura* so much that he stayed in bed on the day of their departure. By the time Abigail noticed, he had missed the flight home. Back home, Abigail's mum contacted lost property, who contacted the ship where the stowaway bear was found. A few more Caribbean cruises and a transatlantic crossing later, and Abigail and Lego Bear were reunited at Carnival House, much to her delight. (*Andrew Sassoli-Walker*)

The Spanish-style Ramblas tapas bar on *Ventura*. (P&O Cruises)

Steve and Angie Hampton with their children Joshua, Daniel and Abigail, pictured in the Tamarind Club, *Ventura*, during their first cruise in early 2011. (*Steve Hampton*)

Ventura, overshadowed by the magnificent mountains of southern Norway, June 2008. (*Gail Oswald*)

Azura 2010

Godmother: Darcey Bussell

Azura arrived in Southampton on 7 April 2010. Her design takes the best from other ships in the P&O Cruises fleet, but with exciting new features such as The Retreat – an alfresco spa terrace designed exclusively for adults, offering treatments under airy cabanas. She is the first P&O Cruises ship to have an outdoor cinema, aptly named SeaScreen. Her cabin décor is more boutique hotel than cruise ship and, in response to customer feedback, has eighteen single cabins. There are eleven different venues in which to eat, including Sindhu under Michelin-starred chef, Atul Kochhar, and the The Glass House, a wine bar and restaurant set up in collaboration with TV wine expert Olly Smith and offering his own selection of wines. Olly also blended P&O Cruises own award-winning house wine.

Andrew Harvey and his partner booked a fly-cruise to the Caribbean on board *Azura*. They were nervous of trying such a large ship as they had only ever sailed on the mid-sized ships before but were pleasantly surprised. 'We experienced outstanding P&O-style service from a bar waiter in the Blue Bar. On the second morning of the cruise he walked past me out on deck and said "Morning Mr Harvey", after having served us one drink the previous evening. By the third night he knew both our names, what we drank and our cabin number. It is great that you can still receive the same wonderful service on these huge ships that we got on little *Victoria* back in 1997! Some of these staff never cease to amaze me.'

Left: Shipyard and P&O Cruises' workers are dwarfed by the stern-thruster housings and one of the twin propellers on *Azura*, 26 June 2009. (P&O Cruises)

Above: At the float-out ceremony for *Azura* at the Monfalcone yard in Italy, 27 June 2009, Amanda Dowds, wife of the ship's master, Captain Keith Dowds, performed the traditional ceremony of laying a coin (in this case a newly minted one pound piece and a new Euro) at the foot of the mast for good luck. A priest then blessed the ship as a bottle Italian sparkling wine was broken against the hull and the dock was flooded for *Azura* to enter the water for the first time. (P&O Cruises)

Opposite: Fincantieri workers painting the name on *Azura*, 26 June 2009. (P&O Cruises)

This page, clockwise from top left: A fire-tug escorts *Azura* as she arrives in Southampton for the first time, 7 April 2010. (*Andrew Sassoli-Walker*)

Ventura sails past *Azura* on the evening of the latter's naming ceremony, 10 April 2010. (*Andrew Sassoli-Walker*)

Azura berthed at the Ocean Terminal in Southampton on the evening of her maiden arrival, 8 April 2010. (*Andrew Sassoli-Walker*)

Opposite, clockwise from top left: An outside single cabin on *Azura*. (P&O Cruises)

The Oasis Pool on *Azura* is part of the Oasis Spa and Health Club. (*Andrew Sassoli-Walker*)

The Retreat is an alfresco spa terrace on *Azura*, designed exclusively for adults, and offering treatments under airy cabanas and beneath moonlit skies. (*Andrew Sassoli-Walker*)

The Planet Bar on *Azura*, where passengers enjoy stunning views from the windows, while behind them a 20-metre plasma video wall screens iconic, man-made and natural wonders from the world's continents. (*Andrew Sassoli-Walker*)

A first for P&O Cruises – the SeaScreen on *Azura*, where films can be enjoyed on deck. (*Andrew Sassoli-Walker*)

Top left: Captain Paul Brown, master of *Azura*. (*Andrew Sassoli-Walker*)

Top right: *Azura* sets sail in the evening sunlight on her maiden voyage – a sixteen-night Mediterranean cruise, 2010. (*Andrew Sassoli-Walker*)

Adonia 2011

Godmother: Dame Shirley Bassey

Adonia is the newest and smallest addition to the P&O Cruises fleet. At 30,000grt she has a small-ship charm and, like *Arcadia* and *Oriana*, is exclusively for adults, carrying just 710 passengers. Built in 2001, she was one of the Renaissance Cruises R class ships. Her first master, Commodore Steve Burgoine, is clearly proud of his latest command. On a smaller ship, he gets to meet everyone, often more than once during a cruise. He can also take *Adonia* to the more unusual and out-of-the-way ports, so she really is the pathfinder of the fleet. He has been in command of most of P&O Cruises' ships, but upon being asked which has been his favourite, he replied, 'Whichever ship I'm in command of at the time!' He commented that amongst all the many stunning ports he has visited around the world, Sydney in Australia rates among his favourites. Life President of P&O Cruises, Lord Sterling presented Commodore Burgoine with a ceremonial sword on the occasion of *Adonia*'s naming, which is displayed near to Reception.

The distinctive main staircase on *Adonia*, 2011. (*Andrew Sassoli-Walker*)

The maiden arrival of *Adonia* at Southampton, 20 May 2011. (*Andrew Sassoli-Walker*)

Right: The spectacular Norwegian Fjords form a backdrop to the sun deck of *Adonia*, June 2011. (*Gail Oswald*)

Left: *Adonia* is greeted by fire tugs on her maiden arrival at Southampton, 20 May 2011. (*Andrew Sassoli-Walker*)

Left: The elegant library on *Adonia*. (*Andrew Sassoli-Walker*)

Above: The Crow's Nest Bar on *Adonia*. (*P&O Cruises*)

Below: Traditional wooden steamer chairs on *Adonia*. (*Andrew Sassoli-Walker*)

Left: Workers and onlookers line the Belfast waterfront at the Harland and Wolff shipyard to witness the launch of *Canberra*, 16 March 1960. Reproduced by Kind Permission of P&O Heritage Collection & P&OSNCo. (*J&C McCutcheon collection*)

Right: Dame Shirley Bassey, naming *Adonia*. (*P&O Cruises*)

Below left: Ceremonial sword presented to Commodore Ian Gibb at the naming ceremony of *Oriana*, 1995. (*Andrew Sassoli-Walker*)

Below right: Ceremonial sword presented to the first captain of *Aurora*, Steve Burgoine, at her naming in 2000. (*Andrew Sassoli-Walker*)

Chapter 6

WHAT'S IN A NAME? – FROM ROYALTY TO CELEBRITY

Often, the names of a fleet of ships give some indication as to which line they belong, for example the 'ic' endings of the White Star Line – *Olympic*, *Majestic* and so on. In the early years of P&O, ship names were generally related to the company's supporters or routes such as *Bentinck*, *Persia*, *Egypt* and *Arabia*. As the fleet grew they moved on to using an alphabetical system for classes of vessels, maintaining consistency by all names ending in a, for example the M class included *Moldavia*, *Malwa* and *Medina*. For the Australian route, B was chosen with, among others, *Beltana* and *Benalla* and N for the Far Eastern station – *Narkunda* and *Naldera*. In 1887, the Jubilee ships entered the fleet. Since this was not only the Golden Jubilee of P&O, but of Queen Victoria as well, two of the ships were given suitably patriotic names – *Britannia* and *Victoria*. The other two were *Oceana* and *Arcadia*. However, geographical names continued well into the 1960s. *Canberra* for example, is the capital city of Australia as well as an aboriginal name generally accepted as meaning a 'meeting place by the water'.

From the start it was common practice that when a favourite ship left the fleet, she would be remembered by the re-use of her name. *Oriana* is just one such example. Such was her importance to the British cruise industry, for reasons previously mentioned, the naming ceremony was no less in magnitude, the honour going to HM the Queen. The name *Oriana* was a name given to Queen Elizabeth I by her courtiers and, when Orient Lines' *Oriana* was introduced in 1959, it was to celebrate the second Elizabethan era. It seemed fitting that the present *Oriana* would celebrate the continuing era of Queen Elizabeth II.

Aurora, the Roman Goddess of the dawn, was appropriate for a ship being introduced at the start of not just a new decade or century, but a new millennium. Her naming ceremony was carried out by HRH The Princess Royal. The then Chairman, Lord Sterling, commented , 'P&O is honoured that The Princess Royal will name *Aurora*, ensuring an auspicious start to the ship's entry into service. It is particularly appropriate as Her Royal Highness is President of the Missions to Seafarers charity.'

In 2003, *Oceana* was also named by HRH the Princess Royal. She is also the second company ship to bear the name, the first being one of the Jubilee ships of 1888. *Oceana*, together with her sister, the first *Adonia* (now *Sea Princess*) were the first vessels ever to have a joint ceremony, when Princess Anne and her daughter, Zara Philips named them in May 2003. P&O Cruises marketed the two ships as the 'White Sisters', a term last used for the *Strath* ships of the 1930s.

Arcadia is a another example of the re-use of a name, the current vessel being the fourth *Arcadia*, built in 2005. She was chosen for a new style of naming ceremony. As the guests stood in a huge marquee at the City Cruise Terminal, the vessel slipped her moorings and took station just off the berth, showcasing the versatility of her azipod propulsion system. Spectacular displays including acrobats entertained the guests and, as Dame Kelly Holmes named the ship, a waterfall of fireworks showered over the bow accompanied by a stunning pyrotechnic display set to Handel's *Zadok the Priest*, familiar as the theme in P&O Cruises TV adverts.

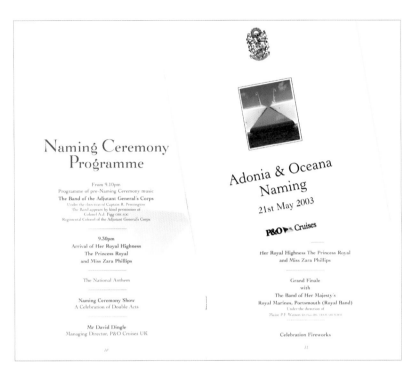

Naming Ceremony Programme

From 9.10pm
Programme of pre-Naming Ceremony music
The Band of the Adjutant General's Corps
Under the direction of Captain R. Pennington
The Band appears by kind permission of
Colonel A.J. Figg OBE ADC
Regimental Colonel of the Adjutant General's Corps

9.30pm
Arrival of Her Royal Highness
The Princess Royal
and Miss Zara Phillips

The National Anthem

Naming Ceremony Show
A Celebration of Double Acts

Mr David Dingle
Managing Director, P&O Cruises UK

Adonia & Oceana Naming
21st May 2003

P&O Cruises

Her Royal Highness The Princess Royal
and Miss Zara Phillips

Grand Finale
with
The Band of Her Majesty's
Royal Marines, Portsmouth (Royal Band)
Under the direction of
Major P.F. Watson BA(Hons) BN, CRSM MO RORM

Celebration Fireworks

Opposite page, clockwise from top left: Souvenir programme for the joint naming ceremony of *Oceana* and *Adonia* (now Sea Princess), 2003. (*Sharon Poole collection*)

Dame Helen Mirren with Royal Marines Alastair Burton and Carl Thurgood, prior to the Naming Ceremony for *Ventura*, 2008. The two commandos abseiled down the side of the ship and smashed the bottle against the hull. (P&O Cruises)

Principal ballerina, Darcey Bussell and Captain Keith Dowds at the naming ceremony of *Azura*, 11 April 2010. (P&O Cruises)

Celebratory fireworks over *Adonia*, following her naming by Dame Shirley Bassey, 21 May 2011. (P&O Cruises)

This page: *Arcadia* held station just off her berth in Southampton for her naming ceremony by Dame Kelly Homes, highlighting her versatile azipod propulsion system which makes her the most manoeuvrable ship in the P&O Cruises fleet. (*Andrew Sassoli-Walker*)

Ventura had a spectacular ceremony with a James Bond style theme. It involved some of the cast members from BBC spy series *Spooks* 'rescuing' the naming trigger, which had been 'stolen' by a villain aptly played by Jonathan Pryce. Once retrieved, it was delivered to Dame Helen Mirren who uttered the time-honoured words to bless the ship and all who sailed in her. She then pressed the button, which sent a team of Royal Marine Commandos abseiling down the bow to smash the bottle of champagne. Dame Helen went on to say, 'When I was a little girl, only the Queen and Princess Margaret launched ships. Tonight, my dreams of becoming a princess have come true – I've met the Royal Marines and Noddy on the same day – how fantastic is that?' The evening was completed by a spectacular firework display. Nigel Esdale, then P&O Cruises Managing Director, commented that, 'We wanted the launch to be as imaginative as the ship herself.'

Azura was named by prima ballerina, Darcey Bussell at a glittering ceremony hosted by Sir Trevor McDonald. Darcey danced on stage prior to Captain Keith Dowds escorting her to the plinth. She used a clapper board to cut a ribbon which sent a bottle of champagne smashing over the funnel followed by clouds of ticker tape and more fireworks. Darcey was so excited at being Godmother that she brought her whole family to the event. Her eight-year-old daughter was delighted when she exclaimed that as Mummy was Godmother, that meant that she and her sister were Goddaughters to the ship and of course Daddy must be the 'Godfather'!

Adonia is the most recent of the ships to join the fleet and although the smallest, had no less a star for her Naming in the Welsh singing legend, Dame Shirley Bassey. Actor Hugh Bonneville was Master of Ceremonies and he spoke of the classical myth of the goddess Venus, her young lover Adonis, and the festival of Adonia. When Adonis died, Venus wept over the loss of her beloved. 'It is said a two-day festival of Adonia was begun in honour of his passing. On the first day all was toil, wailing and tribulation; on the second – joy, celebration and rebirth. Well, the toil of preparing this splendid vessel is over. Today, we celebrate her rebirth as she begins her new life on the high seas.' David Dingle, currently Chief Executive Officer of Carnival UK, has a passion for classical mythology and some of the vessel names reflect this interest, not only in *Adonia* but her predecessor, *Artemis* and of course *Aurora*. At the appropriate moment Dame Shirley pressed a diamond-shaped button to release a bottle of English pink sparkling wine. She later entertained the crowds with an impromptu performance of *Diamonds are Forever*, before introducing the customary firework display, lighting up the Hampshire skyline.

The Needles lighthouse is only seen today by passengers sailing on *Adonia* as she is the sole ship in the current P&O Cruises fleet that can sail through the Western Solent. (P&O Cruises)

Chapter 7

SOUTHAMPTON – A PLACE TO CALL HOME

P&O's links with the Hampshire port of Southampton are nearly as old as the company itself when, in 1840, the Government chose the town as the official UK mail port, although this decision did not properly take effect until 1843. Southampton was chosen as it was reasonably close to London for the transport of the mails and was conveniently placed for sailing south to the Mediterranean. *Oriental* was the first P&O ship to be based in the port. The description in *The Hampshire Advertiser & Salisbury Guardian* of her maiden arrival could almost be describing the arrival of a new cruise liner today, as local people were allowed to look over the vessel. 'She is of a universally admitted beautiful model, and constructed throughout without regard to trouble or expense ... The Saloon with the sleeping rooms attached to it ... occupies the after part of the main deck under the quarter deck ... The Spar Deck (or Upper Deck) affords a superb and uninterrupted promenade, 200 feet in length ... The principal fore cabin is very superior for first-class passengers ... Air and light are copiously admitted ... and the dormitories or berths are amidships, so that the rolling, if any, will scarcely be perceptible. ... The space between them and the vessel's side ... is formed on one side into a tea-room and on the other an equally spacious lounging-room.' Tours of new ships became a regular feature in Southampton when the company introduced a new vessel to their fleet.

The link between P&O and the increasing prosperity of Southampton was highlighted a few months later in the *Morning Post*, April 1841, '... there were also £25,000 of British silver coin, £5,000 foreign silver coin and about £40,000 worth of foreign goods from the bonded warehouses ... Of these goods it may be observed that about £70,000 were exported to the Channel Islands, France and the Mauritius, and the remainder in The Peninsular & Oriental Steam Packet Company's vessels to Lisbon, Gibraltar, Malta and Alexandria. It is to this last important source of communication that we are in a great measure indebted for so rapid a rise in the rank of commercial towns.'

Although the ships still called at Falmouth, Southampton was of increasing importance to their trade. The company was relentless in pushing for improvements to the infrastructure of the port, for example, in 1841 the company's port agent at Southampton requested that the Harbour Commissioners might use the ship's manifest in order to work out harbour dues, 'instead of the harbour-master overhauling the number of baggage'.

Over the next forty years or so, P&O established warehouses, offices, even schools for the children of crew and staff that lived in Southampton. All of which made their decision in 1874 to transfer operations to London that much harder. With the company still suffering from the costs incurred by the opening of the Suez Canal, the decision was taken for commercial reasons alone. Most of the freight carried by P&O was from London shippers who had to bear the cost of transporting their goods to Southampton. Competitors were happy to use London Docks, so the shippers issued an ultimatum – move or they would use rival lines. The ships still continued to call at Southampton until 1881.

In 1903, P&O's home on the Thames was moved again, this time to the Essex town of Tilbury, where a landing stage was built, along with repair facilities located nearby. However, when *Oriana* (1959) and *Canberra* were in the process of building, it was clear Tilbury would be too small to handle these much larger ships, although Tilbury continued to serve P&O until 1969, after which all passenger services moved back once again to Southampton. This time their home was Berth 106 where a new purpose-built cruise terminal was constructed. Rebuilt in 2002, it is known today as the Mayflower Terminal and still welcomes thousands of P&O Cruises' passengers every year.

P&O Cruises' strong links with the city were reinforced when Carnival UK decided to construct their headquarters on the waterfront with a landmark building opened in 2009. The same year, the newest cruise facility in Southampton opened, following a long-term agreement with Associated British Ports. The first ship to berth at the £19 million Ocean Terminal was *Oceana*.

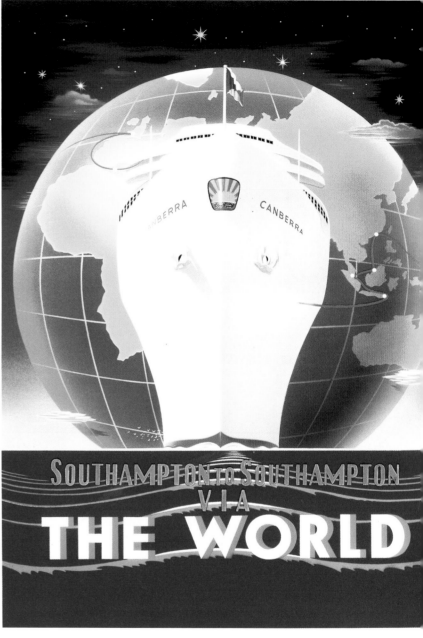

Above left: Southampton's Outer Dock was the first home of P&O in the port. It is now the Ocean Village Marina. (*Andrew Sassoli-Walker*)

Above right: A 1990's advert for *Canberra's* annual world cruise. A world cruise has to be the most convenient and luxurious way of travelling to distant countries. 'Round the World Tours" were listed by P&O as early as 1908, but they involved overland rail travel between different P&O ships. The first world cruise as we know it today was in 1922 on Cunard's *Laconia*. Since then thousands of people have travelled on this most desirable of voyages. Reproduced by Kind Permission of P&O Heritage Collection & P&OSNCo. (*Mark Thomas collection*)

This page: *Arcadia* and *Iberia* off the Needles, Isle of Wight. In 1841, a report was published in the *Hampshire Advertiser & Salisbury Guardian* that Lieutenant Kendall, Marine Superintendent of P&O had written to the Southampton Pier Commissioners about making vital improvements to the navigation aids on the approaches to Southampton Water. 'As the representative of a large and increasing company, owning a considerable amount of tonnage in the constant habit of trading to the port of Southampton, I feel it my bounden duty to bring before your notice the following suggestions ... It is the fact that, although pronounced by competent judges to contain greater capabilities than most other ports, and selected by two of the most extensive steam companies in the world for their head-quarters, Southampton is rendered difficult of access to those very vessels to which her prosperity is indebted ... I would strongly suggest that a floating light should immediately be put on the spit off Calshot Castle; that another should be maintained on board the revenue cutter at the mouth of the Itchen, and lastly, but probably first in point of importance, that the Needles light (which from its being liable from its elevation to be constantly obscured by fog, is worse than useless) should be removed...and placed on the Needles Rocks themselves, as far out as a proper foundation could be found. Were this done, a Commander could shape his course and run with confidence, in thick weather, knowing that he could be certain to see the light on nearing it.' His proposals were passed to Trinity House by the Pier Commissioners. A new Needles lighthouse was built in 1859, in the position recommended by Lieutenant Kendall. A floating light still marks Calshot Spit but since 1987 it has been a buoy (pictured left) while the light-ship that formerly highlighted the spit now lies next to the Ocean Terminal. Carnival House, headquarters of P&O Cruises. (*Andrew Sassoli-Walker, J&C McCutcheon collection & P&O Cruises*)

This page, clockwise from top left: Coloured streamers thrown by passengers trail from *Canberra's* rail over the Band of the Royal Marines, playing at another departure from Southampton. (*Andrew Sassoli-Walker*)

Azura at the Ocean Terminal with the fifteenth century city walls of Southampton in the foreground. Before land was reclaimed to expand the port in the late nineteenth century, the sea used to lap at the base of these walls at high tide. (*Andrew Sassoli-Walker*)

Ocean Cruise Terminal with *Ventura* close to departure, July 2011. (*Sharon Poole*)

All quiet at the Mayflower Cruise Terminal check-in desks, just before embarkation begins and the hall fills with people, 2011. (*Andrew Sassoli-Walker*)

Shore Support & Operations

In 1848, P&O opened their head office at 122 Leadenhall Street, London. The original buildings were replaced by a fourteen-storey modern structure in 1969, but they remained there until the early 1980s, when the P&O head office was moved to Pall Mall while P&O Cruises moved to New Oxford Street. Michael Penney wrote of the Leadenhall office in the late 1950s. 'The customer entrance at the front led into a most elegant and lofty hall, superbly furnished. Around the walls were desks for about eight booking clerks ... In the centre was a waiting area, with armchairs, sofas and tables with the latest magazines ... Prospective passengers were led by a uniformed messenger to a vacant desk, or the waiting area ... Having received details of the customer's requirements, the booking clerk completed a booking slip. This showed sailings, dates and the type of accommodation required, which could range from a first-class de-luxe cabin with its own bathroom to a six-berth tourist-class cabin on the lowest deck ... The messenger then carried the booking slip to the Berthing Section ... This was necessary because the opulence of the booking hall was not repeated outside it and the berthing section consisted of a large cupboard under the stairs, furnished with large bookshelves to accommodate the berthing books ... Even ships of the same class were not identical in their cabin layout so a berthing book for every ship had to be separately printed. There was a separate book for each voyage and bookings could be made two years ahead ... On receiving the booking slip the berthing clerk ... searched for vacant cabins that matched the customer's requirements and price. He then wrote an offer on the booking slip ... Another messenger carried the slip back to the booking clerk, who revealed the offer to the intending passenger.'

Nowadays, booking a cruise is so easy – you pick up a brochure or go online, choose your ship, select an appealing itinerary from among the hundreds on offer, decide your preferred cabin grade and book it. Very few perhaps give a thought to the logistical challenges that go into producing each year's brochures.

In deciding where the ships will sail each year, some forty-five different factors have to be taken into account. Ports alone have to meet several criteria – can it be reached in a reasonable time from the previous port; how far is it to the next port; is there a suitable berth or anchorage; is there enough to do ashore to interest passengers; is there transport for shore excursions; are there port facilities for refuelling, fresh water supplies, refuse disposal. All of this has to be planned months or sometimes years in advance of the brochure print deadlines.

There is a large shore-based operation supporting the sea-going staff, from the new-build department that work on designs for new ships, through the fleet services department with engineering and maintenance staff, marketing, personnel and transport. Anthony Robinson was Fleet Personnel Travel Officer, now retired. 'Sea staff that joined or left at Southampton did so very straight-forwardly, but those who did so at way-ports abroad needed to be looked after in a different way. They had to receive air tickets, be met at airports, transported to a hotel for the night and conveyed the following morning to their appointed ship for embarkation and that's where I came in as Travel Officer. Never in my life have I composed and sent so many telex messages basically instructing our agents abroad to "Meet, Accom, & Convey" sea staff. In the case of *Oriana* (1960-86) at Sydney the crew could number about seventy each way. At San Francisco and other Pacific ports the groups were smaller. To complicate things further, when the sea staff left their ship, some chose to stay awhile on holiday before flying home for the rest of their leave. The cost of their air tickets had to be credited to the port and I had to tell them details of their booking before they left the ship. Mixed in between all these large groups were a few senior officers who needed no assistance when flying out from the UK, but it was much more difficult if they were due to embark at, for example, Nukualofa, in the Pacific. I was very proud that in all my time I never failed an officer by not having him met at an obscure airport, hoteled and conveyed safely to his ship. Having spent so much time within the Fleet Personnel Department, no-one knows better than I how tremendous the staff are aboard the P&O Fleet.'

In the past, the P&O had its own repair docks and workmen. Nowadays most on-going maintenance is done while the ship is in service and only refits and major upgrades require dry-docking. When a ship goes in for planned maintenance it is the Engineering and Maintenance Manager who, with his staff, prepare a list of work to be undertaken, obtain tenders, make recommendations as to where to place the contract and oversee the work while it is being done. Up until the 1970s, every P&O ship had an annual refit, but with modern materials and longer maintenance schedules, it may only be required every few years nowadays.

A selection of brochures of the 1970s and 1980s. Reproduced by Kind Permission of P&OSNCo. (*Mark Thomas collection*)

Turn a-round day

'After the efficient and timely disembarkation of 1,098 well-rested and revitalised passengers, we began to embark yourselves, as well as enormous quantities of food, baggage, fuel and stores to keep the engines turning to be consumed over the next seven days. Our comprehensive pre-departure checks were started upstairs and downstairs (colloquialisms for the bridge and engine room respectively) at 1400 and continued until 1640, when Captain Breton was informed that all pre-departure checks had been completed and that positive reports from the various departments had been received. A short while beforehand, at 1600, our Southampton pilot had boarded and with him complementing the bridge team, all our mooring lines were let go at 1640.'

This is an extract from the log given to passengers at the end of a Christmas Markets cruise on *Artemis*, 14 December 2010.

Turn a-round day and the two days either side are the busiest days for the whole crew. It starts over a year in advance with the confirmation of the dates that each ship will arrive home. Berths are confirmed as there are four cruise terminals in Southampton – Mayflower, City, Queen Elizabeth 2 and the latest Ocean Terminal. Once dates are known, preparations are made with the various suppliers so they can deliver everything to the ship from toilet rolls and food to fuel and flowers.

Pilots are booked to assist in the arrival and departure of each ship and tugs stood by in the event they may be needed, such as in windy conditions. Stevedores are needed for mooring and the attaching of gangways, be they conventional gangways or airport-style air bridges.

As the ship approaches home waters, around 10 miles from the Nab Tower, which is the boarding area for the Southampton pilot, the Officer of the Watch will contact Southampton VTS (Vessel Traffic Services) who control all movements around the Solent. They update the ship with current weather and tide information, what side the pilot will be boarding, ship movements and any other important information. For all arrivals and departures both the captain and deputy captain are on the bridge. Once on board, the pilot will then pass on his local knowledge to the captain to assist in getting the ship safely through the busy traffic lanes and natural hazards. At various points the ship will radio her position to VTS as all radio traffic is recorded along with radar tracks.

As the ship approaches the berth, officers and ratings man the mooring positions and send the lines ashore for stevedores to secure to bollards on the quayside.

Once safely berthed and with the gangways attached, the pilot disembarks and officers from the Port Health Authority and UK Border Agency staff, perhaps more commonly known by their previous name as customs officers, come on board. Port Health officers ensure high standards of hygiene are continually met. UK Border Agency staff are there to clear the ship so that passengers and crew can proceed ashore. Random checks can be carried out to make sure no illegal substances, alcohol or cigarettes are smuggled into the country. Once cleared by the authorities, turnaround day truly begins.

One tradition to show the ship off in port is 'dressing her overall' where a colourful selection of flags are raised from stem to stern. A large Red Ensign, the flag of the British Merchant Navy, will also be flown at the stern. The bunkering barge arrives alongside to refuel the ship, while another ties up to take waste and recyclable materials safely away to be processed.

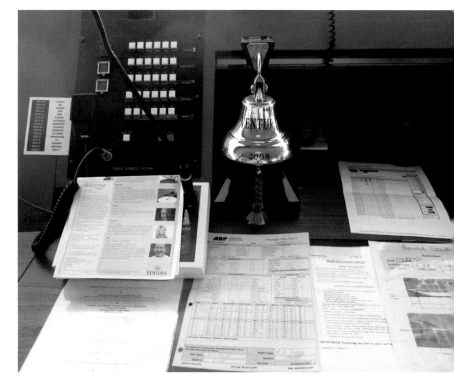

Top: There are four cruise terminals at Southampton – as *Adonia* arrives for the first time (hence the fire tugs) to berth at Mayflower Terminal, *Oriana* is already moored at City Terminal (left) and *Ventura* at Ocean Terminal, 20 May 2011. The fourth is QEII Terminal. (*Andrew Sassoli-Walker*)

Bottom: The ship's bell on the bridge of *Ventura*, together with various documentation for her arrival home to Southampton, 2011. (*Sharon Poole*)

Clockwise from top left: Captain David Box berths *Artemis* at Southampton, with assistance from the local pilot and deputy captain, whilst the stevedores bring the lines ashore. *(Andrew Sassoli-Walker)*

Crew raising the flags to dress *Adonia* overall on a turnaround day in Southampton, August 2010. *(Sharon Poole)*

The Red Ensign of the British merchant fleet is flown in every port. This is *Artemis* at Zeebrugge. *(Andrew Sassoli-Walker)*

The evening before arrival, luggage is collected from outside cabins and stored overnight in areas on the lower decks. It is sent ashore in cages and arranged in the Luggage Hall in deck order by porters so passengers can locate their suitcases.

Lorry-loads of stores are brought to the dockside to begin the major task of restocking the ship from top to bottom – shampoo to sugar, light bulbs to lettuces – so the vessel is as self-sufficient as possible. Modern cruise ships usually carry sufficient stocks for the current cruise plus a few days extra in case of delays. Stores Manager on *Azura*, Victor Venturini, described his job, 'An average working day can involve anything from taking on stores to checking freezer rooms. Our busiest day is in Southampton when we do a full loading averaging about 250-300 tonnes of stores to get on board and stow. After that we start to issue goods to our various outlets for dinner and breakfast the following day. The most challenging part of the job is the ordering process. Trying to determine what passengers are going to eat and drink during a standard two-week cruise is a big challenge as it can vary by itinerary and time of year.'

On board, passengers enjoy their last breakfast and patiently wait for the call to disembark. Meanwhile, the stewards are busy stripping beds, cleaning bathrooms, replenishing toiletries, laying out new information folders and generally getting cabins ready for the new arrivals.

There may be a change-over of crew as well as passengers. It is a complicated task to co-ordinate a crew change, ensuring transfers to airports and the necessary flights to all corners of the globe, while the same has to be arranged for those embarking. A shuttle bus operates between the terminal and the city centre for anyone who has time off during the busy day.

Once passengers are all on their way home, an air of calm descends on the public areas, but the buzz of activity continues as the ship is readied for the new influx. Flowers will be delivered; contractors may come on board to relay carpet, or repair equipment; a piano tuner checks all the pianos on board (most of the ships have around five grand pianos). Loyalty Managers will be checking lists to see how many Portunus Club members there will be on the forthcoming cruise as invitations have to go out for parties, etc. (this will change to the Peninsular Club in April 2012). Meanwhile, visitors may have come on tours of the ship to see what a P&O Cruises holiday can offer.

At midday, the check-in desks within the terminal building start receiving the first passengers. Once checked-in and scanned through security they are allowed to board. They could be eating lunch in the

Above left: Luggage awaiting reclamation by passengers at the Mayflower Cruise Terminal, 2011. (*Sharon Poole*)

Above right: Loading luggage onto the ship at the Ocean Terminal. (*Andrew Sassoli-Walker*)

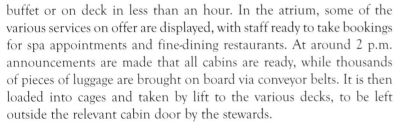

buffet or on deck in less than an hour. In the atrium, some of the various services on offer are displayed, with staff ready to take bookings for spa appointments and fine-dining restaurants. At around 2 p.m. announcements are made that all cabins are ready, while thousands of pieces of luggage are brought on board via conveyor belts. It is then loaded into cages and taken by lift to the various decks, to be left outside the relevant cabin door by the stewards.

Gradually the terminal becomes silent, lorries disappear and passengers sip their first drinks as the air of anticipation and excitement starts to build. The pilot embarks, ready to assist in taking the ship out to sea, the mooring gangs standby and various checks are carried out whilst the captain makes the announcements at the regulatory muster

drill for all passengers. This ensures everyone is familiar with what to do in the unlikely event of an emergency.

On the quayside a band starts to play and once muster drill is over, passengers congregate on deck for the sail-away party. Any remaining shore staff and contractors disembark and the gangways are disconnected. The pilot then announces his departure over the radio to VTS (Vessel Traffic System) confirming draft, next port and the number of passengers and crew on board. The officer at VTS will advise of any ship arrivals or departures that they need to be aware of.

The captain comes over the tannoy once more, 'Good afternoon ladies and gentlemen. All our pre-departure safety checks have been satisfactorily carried out and we are ready to put to sea. My crew and I wish you a most memorable cruise.' The ship 'singles up' with only two lines ashore, then when the 'let go all' is ordered, all lines are released and the ship is finally away. The traditional three blasts of the ship's whistle signal to both those on board and to the well-wishers ashore that the cruise has well and truly begun.

Once the ship transits Southampton Water and the Solent and disembarks the pilot, turn-around day is over, until the next time. With all seven ships berthing at Southampton over 150 times a year, this operation is often taken for granted, a testimony to the efficiency of all concerned.

Opposite, clockwise from top left: Rachel Caddick, Food & Beverage Operations Manager, and Victor Venturini, Hotel Stores Manager, *Azura*, July 2011. (*Andrew Sassoli-Walker*)

Crew members restocking the temperature-controlled vegetable storeroom on *Azura*. (*Sharon Poole*)

Stores being loaded onto *Adonia* at the Mayflower Cruise Terminal, 2011. (*Andrew Sassoli-Walker*)

This page, clockwise from top left: Engineers servicing the drinks machines in the Belvedere buffet restaurant on *Arcadia*, on a turn-around day, August 2011. (*Sharon Poole*)

The Piano Bar on *Arcadia*, at the top of the atrium. There are approximately five pianos on each ship in the fleet. (*Andrew Sassoli-Walker*)

Newly-embarked passengers at Reception on *Azura*. (*Andrew Sassoli-Walker*)

Ventura departs for the Norwegian Fjords, 16 July 2011. (Sharon Poole)

Southampton Water can be very busy. Here, HMS *Illustrious* and the Clipper Round-the-World yachts pass *Aurora* heading to the start line for the race, July 2011. The VTS (Vessel Traffic Services) staff ensure all vessels enter and leave port safely with regular communication. (*Andrew Sassoli-Walker*)

Oceana follows *Arcadia* down Southampton Water on the day of *Arcadia's* maiden voyage, April 2005. (*Andrew Sassoli-Walker*)

Technology

Computers and information technology are so much part of life today that it is hard to comprehend the amount of work required in running a shipping company before they arrived. It wasn't so long ago when a passenger had to take cash or travellers' cheques and everything bought on board, from a glass of wine to souvenirs, had to be paid for at the time. Nowadays it is as simple as registering a credit or debit card at check-in. The passenger is then issued with a cruise card, which, on the newest ships, is not only used for purchases, but also as cabin key and identity card for getting on and off the ship.

Dealing with the IT side is a mammoth task and Niel Hillawi is one such person who has taken up this challenge. Based at Carnival House. He writes, 'Information technology sits at the heart of a P&O Cruises ship and underpins just about every function or operation, be it navigation, engine and power management to maintenance of passenger folios and on board spend. Each time there is a technological revolution in the world of media and communications, there is an expectation that these means are available on board. Passengers take it for granted that they can phone home, surf the internet or attend meetings using their mobile phone whilst half way across the seas.

IT has been around a long time but the 1980s saw the development of the first practical modern computer systems for managing passenger folios. However, to get the data tapes containing the reservations details to the ships involved people carrying suitcases, sometimes half way around the world.

The 1990s saw the introduction of satellite communication supporting data transmissions. These data tapes were now sent electronically. The enhancement in communications also opened the door to email, direct access to reservations, credit card authentication, etc. All of a sudden, the world got a whole lot smaller. The late 1990s also saw the removal of the dependency on cash for all but crew pay and foreign currency exchange and led to greater controls of sales and inventory management.

Today, the whole ship is alive with innovative features for passengers and crew giving the appearance of an effortless lifestyle. The pace of this development is matched closely to the availability of new products on the market.

Almost every conceivable type of IT-driven service can be found on a P&O Cruises ship in one way or another. There are very few industries that match this breadth. Behind this amazing on board technology is a well-oiled machine of highly skilled support technicians, analysts/project

Above: The new cyber-study on *Arcadia*, August 2011. Every P&O Cruises' ship has an area where passengers may access the internet and emails. All the ships also offer Wi-fi in selected areas, with *Adonia* and *Azura* Wi-fi throughout. (*Sharon Poole*)

Below: The Den on *Ventura* offers all the latest video and computer games. (*Andrew Sassoli-Walker*)

Technology is an integral part of life today, whether for research, booking a cruise, reading blogs, viewing webcams of the fleet, or sharing stories. (*Andrew Sassoli-Walker*)

managers and system developers based in Southampton. They keep a close eye on the innovations as they evolve and work out how to knit these often very different systems together into what looks like a cohesive integrated solution for the benefit of our passengers and crew.'

When considering a cruise some twenty years ago, one would pick up a brochure, following an advert either on television or in a magazine or newspaper. Nowadays with webcams, social media, blogs and all manner of material on the Internet, one can virtually experience a cruise before leaving the house!

With other brands in the Carnival group starting to write web logs (known now as 'blogs'), Micky Arison approached P&O Cruises suggesting they get something underway. An executive purser seemed the ideal choice as they are involved in so many aspects of a cruise and one name kept coming up, James Cusick. Excited by the prospect, he set about writing his first blog whilst serving on *Arcadia*. What no one realised at the time was quite how popular this would become! The first blog entry was written in October 2008 – 'Greetings from the P&O Cruises ship *Arcadia*. We are currently at sea and I am

sitting here in the executive purser's office at 2200 hours getting to grips with the blog! I do hope that as it gets underway we have many laughs and good memories to share. We have just left Civitavecchia which is the ancient port of Rome – all roads lead to Rome! Over 1,200 passengers enjoyed wonderful excursions in Italy ... The show tonight in The Palladium Theatre is "World Steps" performed by our own Headliners Theatre Company who have just received a standing ovation at their first sitting show – fantastic! ... Passengers are amazed at the energy of our show company and just love it. Even better when 750 passengers made the effort to attend after a long day – and with the theatre packed to capacity, a sure testament to our production shows! Most likely a quiet night will follow for many to rest up as we cruise overnight on our way to Palau ... Good Night! James.'

By July 2011, there were 459 entries and it has seen readers taken to all four corners of the virtual world. It has proved so popular James was nominated for 'best blogger' at the annual Cruise International Awards, 2011. In the future, there are plans to evolve the blog into something new and exciting, so watch this space!

Chapter 8

WHAT DEFINES 'P&O-NESS'?

'For a Briton, it is a thing of proper pride to travel in a fine British ship. We are not, maybe, so mighty as we were, but the Red Ensign of the British Merchant Fleet still flutters over all the oceans and commands respect in every port of the world.' So wrote Sir Alan Herbert in the introduction of his book, *All About Cruising* in 1959. He continued, 'You should see what a stir they [the ships] make when they come in and when they go. They wear such an air of beauty and cleanliness, of discipline and smooth efficiency, well-designed and built, well-managed and handled. Wherever they are seen there is no more talk of Britain as a declining power with nothing but a past. They show the flag and win us praise as no statesman, no sportsman, nor even perhaps the aircraft can.'

P&O Cruises Managing Director, Carol Marlow first used the term 'P&O-ness' in 2010 to describe that special atmosphere on a P&O Cruises ship. 'Our passengers particularly love the way we tailor everything to their British needs; the way we actually celebrate being on a ship, with the officers and crew making this a real nautical experience, as only we can, due to the fact we can trace our roots back longer than any other cruise line. They also love the way that a cruise with us is a special occasion that they will remember for a long time to come.'

An early visitor to *Canberra* put it perfectly. 'There is one last thing I should mention which I sensed again as soon as I stepped on board and which I have never felt on any ship of another line on which I have travelled. It is hard to define what it is; passengers in my time would comment upon it; it might be described as an atmosphere of discipline and orderliness. On the other hand, it may be that, although I feel it is something more, it is a mystique the P&O have, and I hope the company will always keep it.'

The reputation of P&O was recognised even in the nineteenth century. F. Kendall wrote in a letter to his mother in 1859, 'When we were going into Gib, the little *Alhambra* was lying at anchor and flying a pennant as the Admiralty Agent was on board. One of the passengers was looking at her and asked what war steamer that was. Oh, said I, that is the *Alhambra*, she only flies the pennant because there is a Lieutenant in the Navy on board. "Nonsense," said he, "you never see a merchant steamer's rigging in such order as that". Really, speaking without prejudice, if you do see a P&O steamer alongside that of any other merchant steamer, I don't care what service, you will see the difference directly.' P&O staff often quoted their old maxim that 'There is the Royal Navy, the P&O and the Merchant Navy'

Edwin Arnold also put it well in his book *India Revisited* in 1886, 'It would be ungrateful in the last degree not to speak in terms of warm praise of the ship, her officers and the general management of the voyage ... The country has reason to be proud of such a company as the Peninsular & Oriental which keeps in constant and perfect service this floating bridge of regular and well-ordered communication to its eastern empire.'

From the start P&O captains were usually recruited from the Royal Navy. Their word was, literally, law and they ran their ships with naval discipline and a calm control which rubbed off on the crews, who

Clockwise from top left: The Best of British! *Azura* just visible though a Red Ensign of the British Merchant fleet. (*Andrew Sassoli-Walker*)

The sleek curves of the bow of *Oceana*, flying the P&O Cruises' house flag, pictured from the starboard bridge wing. (*Andrew Sassoli-Walker*)

Canberra – looking shipshape and Bristol fashion, the epitome of the P&O ethos. (*Andrew Sassoli-Walker*)

Strathmore, dressed overall, in Southampton's Western Docks in the 1950s. (J&C McCutcheon collection)

had no doubt in their minds that 'P&O was best'. This self-belief and confidence in the quality of their product spread not only to all the ships, but to the shore stations, hotels and offices throughout the world. Passengers liked the warm welcome, comfortable surroundings and the attentive but not obsequious service.

A passenger was moved to write to the Chairman, Sir Thomas Sutherland, in 1913, 'The splendid steamer *Medina* in which I have made the long voyage to and from Australia is an ideal ship with an ideal Captain, excellent officers, a really good, thoughtful Purser, and first class cook ... The secret of the high estimation in which the P&O Company is held may be attributed to various causes. In the first place passengers feel safer than in any other British steamship company because of the good officers, well-trained, well-disciplined and thoroughly alert and obedient.'

It was put another way in the diary of a young passenger in the 1950s, 'At 6 p.m. we steamed into Naples and I never felt so proud of being British in my life ... We were the best ship in the harbour, the pride of Great Britain ...'

Below: Captain Rhodes of *Mongolia*. P&O uniforms were originally based on the Royal Naval version – so much so in fact that the Admiralty complained to P&O about the issue in 1846. (J&C McCutcheon collection)

Bottom right: The first-class lounge on *Carthage* (1931-61), perfectly illustrating the comfortable rather than overtly luxurious décor of P&O ships. (J&C McCutcheon collection)

Captain Baillie boarded *Stratheden* as a passenger shortly after the end of the Second World War. He wrote of, 'the rows of stewards in their spotless white jackets drawn up and waiting to take your hand luggage; the glistening white paint of the superstructure towering above you; and the long-forgotten atmosphere of solid luxury and willing service ready to engulf you as soon as you stepped over the gangway and into the foyer.'

While P&O never faced the kind of competition that forced lines on the North Atlantic route to build ships of ever increasing luxury, they never allowed the standards set by Willcox and Anderson back in 1837 to drop. Over the years, captains and pursers were deluged with written instructions as to how passengers should be treated and how officers should behave. Junior officers began as cadets and were trained from the start in the ethos of P&O, which not only included seamanship but also attitude and presentation. Michael Penney recalls his first posting as fourth officer to the *Canton* in 1948. 'My uniform wardrobe was the worse for wear after a year in the *Paringa* (a refrigerated cargo ship on the Australia run) and I needed a great deal of clothing for a peace-time passenger ship … The least I could order was a new blue uniform, plus cap and shoes, a mess undress – jacket, waistcoat and trousers – four long white uniform suits, plus shoes, white mess jackets and cummerbund, and last but not least, a lounge suit.'

Sam Brown and her partner, Gordon Vinnicombe, are regular passengers and, when asked what they feel makes P&O Cruises different

from other lines, they highlighted two factors which bring them back time and time again. 'From the moment of booking, to arriving in Southampton, to boarding the ship, to the cruise, to disembarking, the way P&O Cruises make each and every passenger feel special is no mean feat. Plus the crew go out of their way to be helpful, they are friendly and nothing seems to be too much trouble.' Sam went on to mention a cruise on board *Arcadia* in 2006, 'On the first day at sea we shared a table with a young couple and chatted; by the end of the evening we had become friends and six years on we are still friends. We had our anniversary on board and other than booking breakfast in our cabin hadn't planned much else. However, our new friends joined us for a meal. They had been on first sitting and we were on second, but we spoke to the Maître d' who arranged for us to have a table together. It was a very special anniversary which we will always treasure.'

Andrew Myers first started travelling with P&O Cruises in 2006. 'Realising that I would have to go it alone if I ever wanted to cruise, I plumped for P&O Cruises. So off I set on *Oceana* and what a ball I had. Within the first day I had got to know everyone at my table at dinner, went along (with some trepidation) to the Travelling Alone meeting and made loads of new friends. It was the attention to detail that made the cruise so wonderful. I was hooked and within two weeks of getting off, I had booked another. I travelled again on *Oceana*, this time preparing for the post-cruise blues (a condition recognised by deep depression setting in on disembarkation) by already having another booked before I sailed (the only cure). That was *Ventura's* maiden voyage, which was followed by the same on *Azura*. I love the large ships as none of the detail is lost and they still retain the comfort, style and friendliness that I have grown to know and love. I have thought long and hard about why I keep returning to P&O Cruises and it simply boils down to reliability, comfort, warmth of the crew and their ability to be consistently good at all times; ships which meet all of my expectations and with a sense of coming home each time you get on board. You are made to feel special and there is a British-ness about the brand which is always welcome.'

It is their heritage of expertise that has led to P&O Cruises describing themselves as the 'trusted cruise experts'. The company is dedicated to the UK market. Their passengers, ninety-nine per cent of whom are British, think of the ships as a 'home away from home.' They like the fact that the on board currency is sterling, there are touches they recognise and appreciate not least that English is the only language throughout the ships.

Top: Medina (1911-17), which carried King George V and Queen Mary to the Delhi Durbar in India in 1911, shown here at Greenock, which is still a P&O port of call, just before commencing her voyage to Delhi. (*J&C McCutcheon collection*)

Bottom: Aurora, dressed overall and flying the flag for Britain, while berthed at Copenhagen overnight on one of the popular Christmas markets' cruises, December 2008. (*Sharon Poole*)

This page, clockwise from top : Officers on Maloja (1923-54) pose for an official photograph. (J&C McCutcheon collection)

There is no need for anyone to worry that Santa won't find them if they are on a cruise, as he emerges from the funnel of Oriana, to the delight of children and adults alike, Christmas 2010. (Jeanette Fluellen)

Water droplets on the traditional varnished teak handrail on Oceana. (Andrew Sassoli-Walker)

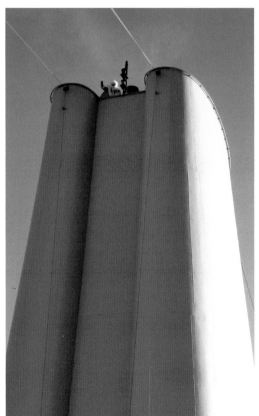

Chapter 9

EVERY MEAL A BANQUET

'Every dinner a banquet, every waiter, a movie star!'

It is hard to define why food becomes so all-important when cruising. Probably it is because, in the early days of long-distance voyages, meals provided some relief from the boredom and a regular time every day to get together with fellow passengers and of course, there is the well-known fact that sea air stimulates the appetite.

In the nineteenth century P&O included all food and drink, including alcoholic beverages, within first-class fares. They were particularly proud of their claret, to the extent of inviting potential passengers to sample it at their London offices. Meals were substantial, beginning with breakfasts of cold meats, kedgeree, eggs and bacon and hot rolls, with tea, coffee or pale ale to drink. Lunch was usually bread or biscuits and cheese, accompanied by wine, spirits or ale. Dinner, served around 3 p.m., was the culinary highlight of the day with soup, boiled chicken, roasted veal, beef, duck and goose and all kinds of cold meats. Dessert was cheese, celery and fresh or dried fruit. The meal was accompanied by unlimited wine, beer, porter and, twice a week, champagne. At 6 p.m. there was tea and at 9 p.m., 'biscuits and grog'. These menus didn't vary, whether you were sailing the Bay of Biscay in winter or the Indian Ocean in summer. The food was staunchly British in flavour with the exception of the famous P&O curries. Introduced when the Indian Station was opened in 1842, these have featured on every menu since and are still a favourite choice on a P&O Cruises ship today. Captain Columb RN wrote, while sailing as a passenger in 1868, 'Those who have not travelled P&O will probably say, how very weak you must be to allow yourself to be commanded by the bell to eat when you know it is not good for you!. Those who have so travelled will not make such a remark!'

In 1871 the complimentary alcoholic drinks policy ended. A bar was set up in the saloon using a cashless system not unlike today. A Company Circular to pursers in January 1871 instructed that, 'Barmen must take charge of all bottles only partly consumed and keep them at the passengers' disposal. He will be furnished with a supply of numbered corks corresponding with the number of berths to prevent mistakes in the re-issuing of wine. No money will be received at the bar, but passengers and officers will be furnished with tickets to fill up with whatever they require, and accounts must be settled weekly. In the event of non-payment of a passenger's wine bill you are authorised to retain such passenger's baggage; but you must exercise your discretion in not having recourse to this step when you believe the passenger's credit may be relied upon.'

In the days before refrigeration, food supplies were limited to whatever could be safely stored. Fresh meat would not have lasted long so live animals were carried, together with hay and grain to feed them. On *Oriental* (1840-1861), 'Half of the top-gallant forecastle is fitted up for the sheep and pigs, so that, being at the extreme end of the vessel, no disagreeable smell is perceptible by the passengers.'

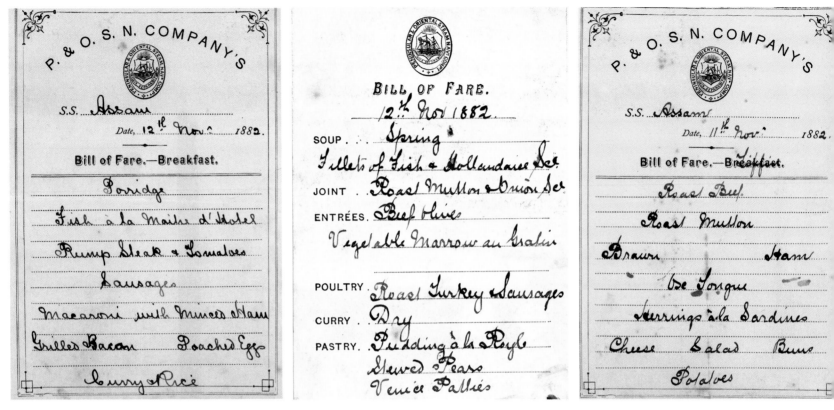

Hand-written menus for breakfast, dinner and tiffin on *Assam*, 1882. An interesting choice for breakfast includes rump steak and macaroni with minced ham. Tiffin was a cross between lunch and afternoon tea and originated in British India. (*J&C McCutcheon collection*)

By 1913 most P&O ships were fitted with refrigerated storage, 'into which it was so dangerous to enter that the duty had to be entrusted to one man only, who had to take infinite precautions beforehand, wearing double thick woollen and flannel clothing before he set foot in that still place bound in the grip of eternal frost' as G.E. Mitton wrote in his book *Peeps at Great Steamship Lines, The P&O*, 1913. He went on to say that approximately half the cargo space was given over to such storage and that, 'The day of Irish stew, ginger snaps and porridge, which, according to a writer in *The Times*, formed the staple of the old diet on a passenger ship, is long past.' P&O prided themselves on providing plenty of food, but equally it was important to minimise waste. The purser was the man responsible for provisioning. Company instructions dictated that, 'It is not the first object of your work to keep down expenditure, but it is your first duty to see a table of superior

quality maintained on board your ship, and your passengers thoroughly well satisfied.' The Directors knew that the company's reputation lay not just with safety, speed and accommodation, but good food. On the 10,990 ton *Morea* (1908-30), they had two galleys – one for first-class and one for second-class passengers. While the quality was the same, there was a greater choice in first-class. The galleys were fitted with every modern convenience of the day including automatic dishwashers.

By the 1950s, the purser had a whole sub-department in charge of catering. The deputy purser was responsible to his manager for the hotel and catering side and directly under him were the chef and chief steward. The chef held responsibility for providing varied menus, along with all preparation, cooking and proper storage of foodstuffs, while managing his staff of cooks, bakers, butchers and storekeepers. From the passenger's viewpoint nothing had changed,

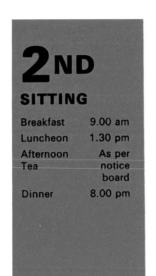

2ND SITTING

Breakfast	9.00 am
Luncheon	1.30 pm
Afternoon Tea	As per notice board
Dinner	8.00 pm

First Class Restaurant

MR. & MRS. M. WHITTINGHAM

Name

D12   25

Cabin No.   Table No.

P. & O. s.s. "STRATHAIRD."
Monday, 14th June, 1937.

LUNCHEON

Bressane Soup
Salmon, Ravigote Sauce
Irish Stew
Welsh Rarebit
Singapore Curry
Grill - Sheeps' Kidneys and Bacon to Order
COLD
Ribs of Beef
Ox Tongue   Melton Mowbray Pie
SALADS
Potato Mixed Spring Onions Cucumber
VEGETABLES
Butter Beans
POTATOES   Baked Lyonnaise Garfield
SWEETS
French Pancakes
Almond Blancmange
Vanilla Cream Ices
Apples   Oranges
CHEESE
Dutch Cream Gorgonzola Bodalla Camembert

Right: Restaurant allocation card for a cruise on *Iberia*, 1968. At this date, second sitting also meant set times for breakfast and lunch as well as dinner. Reproduced by Kind Permission of P&OSNCo. (*Michael Whittingham collection*)

Far right: Tourist-class luncheon menu from *Strathaird*, 1937. Reproduced by Kind Permission of P&OSNCo. (*Sharon Poole collection*)

as one lady wrote in 1959, 'I will conclude with a smiling grumble; the waistband of my slacks appears in some mysterious way to have shrunk by the length of a large safety pin in the last three weeks!'

By then the ships were running two sittings, not only for dinner but for all meals. First sitting was breakfast 8.15 a.m., lunch 12.30 p.m. and dinner 7 p.m. Second sitting was breakfast 9 a.m., lunch 1.30 p.m. and dinner at 8 p.m. There was no buffet restaurant, although Michael Whittingham recalls that on *Chusan* the pool-side cafes would sometimes put on a deck buffet or barbeque at lunch.

Not until the *Strath* ships of the 1930s, was there a choice of table size in the restaurant. However, the biggest change in dining came with *Canberra*. Mark Engelbreston, now working for Carnival UK, sailed on *Canberra* many times as a child and did a school project on the ship in 1990. One of his comments then was that 'the food served is great, there are five-course lunches and seven-course dinners and food is served in different parts of the ship continuously throughout the day.' Michael Longhurst, now retired from P&O Cruises, was travelling in a working capacity on a cruise aboard *Canberra* and was sitting at his table in the restaurant at dinner. 'It was about the third night of the cruise. Sitting at an adjacent table was a family of four consisting of father, a ruddy-faced Yorkshireman, mother and two children. Halfway through the meal the Maitre d' strolled past and stopped at their table. "Is everything all right?" he enquired. "No, it bloody isn't" came the

reply. At this point I noticed the blood drain from the Maitre d's face. "What seems to be the problem?" he asked. "I'll tell thee what the problem is, lad" said he. "I like complaining, see, but there's nowt all to complain about!"'

Nowadays, there are consistent menu cycles across the whole P&O Cruises fleet. Ordering food for each cruise is the joint responsibility of the Food and Beverage Manager and the Executive Chef in liaison with the Stores Manager. In addition to catering for normal menus, some passengers have dietary restrictions or special needs. Stores Manager on *Azura*, Victor Venturini, 'A special diet is easily catered for if we have the correct information sent prior to the required cruise.' Vegetarian choices prove popular and the times are long past when there was just nut roast or mushroom risotto on offer. Sam Brown and her partner enjoy many cruises, 'Speaking as a vegetarian I find a cruise makes my life so much easier. If we go abroad I don't know what I am eating. P&O Cruises always make sure they meet my needs. It's almost like being at home.'

Frequent passengers Nicola Thomas and her children James and Zoë have coeliac disease, which requires a gluten-free diet. Their experience is that the head waiter will advise them which dishes are suitable or order an alternative. On a recent cruise the waiters even anticipated their arrival at afternoon tea with a selection of gluten-free cakes ready and waiting.

Even the best planning can't always get it right! Michael Miles was

Above: The Pacific Restaurant on *Canberra*. (*Andrew Sassoli-Walker*)

Right: Supplies of fresh fruit arrive to be loaded on board. (*Steve Matthews*)

serving as assistant purser on *Arcadia* in 1956. He remembers one cruise when the ship was sailing full and, 'it was quite obvious that in first-class, money was no object. The ship ran out of Krug champagne and smoked salmon and fresh supplies had to be air-freighted to Cannes in order to satisfy the demand.' Even on a recent cruise Victor Venturini recalled, everyone wanted bananas, so for the following cruise he ordered extra supplies, only to discover that the newly embarked passengers all wanted apples!

Always innovative, P&O Cruises introduced a new dining concept with the launch of *Arcadia* in 2005 when they invited a celebrity chef, Gary Rhodes, to open his own restaurant. This was very popular with passengers and was soon followed on *Ventura* with The White Room by Marco Pierre White. Marco now has signature restaurants on *Aurora* (Café Bordeaux), *Oceana* (Café Jardin) and Ocean Grills on *Arcadia*, *Oriana* and *Adonia*. He commented, 'When I sit in the Ocean Grill and see passengers walk through the door, what's beautiful is that there is every age group and they are all there for something different, some are celebrating, some are being romantic, some are just sneaking off to have a quiet dinner and there is something for everybody'. Marco was fascinated by ships from a young age, so was delighted when P&O Cruises approached him and invited him to take a short cruise. He quickly fell under its spell. He recognises the important role food plays in cruising, his main aim being that when people leave one of his signature restaurants, they leave on a high, feeling that they have been looked after.

Azura saw another celebrity chef in Atul Kochhar, who introduced Sindhu, where diners can experience modern Indian cuisine with a British twist. In collaboration with TV wine expert Olly Smith, P&O Cruises also introduced The Glass House. In this wine bar an innovative system allows passengers to sample vintage wines by the glass, each expertly chosen by Olly to accompany the grilled steaks and seafood on offer.

Food trends have changed over the years as passengers become more adventurous about eating ethnic food. New on the menus for 2012 is a taste of local cuisine, serving regional dishes matched to the destinations.

Darren and Mairead Deegan are one of the few married couples serving on board ship. Darren is premier sous chef on *Azura* and Mairead is the senior sous chef. The couple met during their two-year catering course and worked together in Ireland where they finished their training. They have both worked in country house hotels and fine-dining restaurants before joining P&O Cruises together as first commis chefs in 1998. They initially came for one contract but enjoyed it so much that they stayed, moving up through the ranks to the positions they hold today. They said, 'We have had the opportunity to travel the world and work together which has been a great experience for us both.'

Darren went on to describe an average day for him. 'First thing, the executive chef and I walk around the galleys to meet the staff coming on duty and discuss any issues or challenges encountered by the night production teams who are signing off. I am in charge of galley crew changes so I have a few emails to answer each morning from the Mumbai office and Carnival House to ensure we get the correct staff to replace those going on leave. All section heads meet with the senior sous chef each morning to discuss the day's menus. At 10 a.m. every morning I have a meeting with the restaurant managers and head waiters to discuss the previous day's service and any passenger feedback. I then check all the outlets and ensure production is ready for lunch and that the buffet presentation is correctly set up and checked off by the sous chef in charge. Dinner is our busiest time of the day with three restaurants in operation as well as our select dining outlets. We have a chef's tasting table each evening with all the dishes on the menu for dinner from starter, mains, dessert and bread selection. We discuss the menu with the restaurant team and section heads and answer any queries from the head waiters, so they all know what the dishes consist of. During dinner we ensure all dishes go out looking as they should.'

Most of *Azura*'s meals are prepared in her two huge main galleys on decks five and six. The crew galley and mess are also located on deck five. On deck four is the butcher's shop and fish and vegetable preparation rooms as well as the chilled rooms and stores, which hold the vast quantities of food and provisions needed for a cruise.

Statistics reveal some amazing facts. The galleys on *Azura* produce over 13,000 meals every day for the 3,100 passengers and 1,226 crew. This is undertaken by the executive chef and his 165 galley staff. On an average fourteen-day cruise *Azura*'s passengers and crew will consume twenty tons of meat, ten tons of fish, eighty tons of fresh fruit and vegetables, three tons of cheese, 3,500 litres of ice cream, 12,000 yogurts, 120,000 milk portions and 365,000 sachets of jam, sugar and sauces. Over 86,000 eggs, twelve and a half tons of flour and 15,000 litres of milk and cream will be used. 16,000 rolls, 700 loaves of bread and 500 pizzas will be baked every day. All this will be washed down with 12,648 litres of bottled water, 2,850 bottles of wine, 7,200 cans of beer, 4,908 litres of draught beer and 10,000 cans of soft drinks.

Next page, left: Celebrity chef Marco Pierre White, on the dining terrace of *Ventura's* White Room restaurant. (P&O Cruises)

Next page, right: A meal with a view – The Orchid Restaurant on *Arcadia* – superbly situated at the top of the ship. (*Andrew Sassoli-Walker*)

Left: Atul Kochhar's signature restaurant Sindhu on *Azura*. (*Andrew Sassoli-Walker*)

Right: The Glass House, a wine bar and restaurant on *Azura,* created in partnership with wine expert Olly Smith. (*Andrew Sassoli-Walker*)

Opposite, clockwise from left: Darren Deegan (premier sous chef) with his wife Mairead (senior sous chef), *Azura*, July 2011. (*Andrew Sassoli-Walker*)

Tempting lunch-time deserts in the Waterside buffet restaurant on *Ventura*. (*Sue Veale*)

Attention to detail shows in the presentation of after-dinner desserts. (*Sue Veale*)

This page: Lunch-time salads are prepared in *Azura*'s galley for newly-embarked passengers. (*Andrew Sassoli-Walker*)

Clockwise from top left: The Moorish-themed Medina restaurant on *Aurora*. This is one of two main restaurants, the other being the Egyptian-themed Alexandria. (*Andrew Sassoli-Walker*)

Gingerbread village. One of these elaborate creations is built every Christmas on each of the ships. The pastry chefs spend days making each part, and then assemble it overnight. This one was on *Artemis*, Christmas 2010. (*Sharon Poole*)

A talented crew member shows off his ice carving skills on *Arcadia*. (*Sam Brown*)

Opposite: Chocoholics Buffet, *Artemis*, Christmas 2010. One of these afternoon events is usually held on most cruises, and gives the pastry chefs the opportunity to showcase their skills. (*Sharon Poole*)

Aurora at Eidfjord, Norway, dwarfed by the surrounding mountains, June 2009. (Bob Walker)

Chapter 10

GOING ASHORE

For many people it is sufficient just to be at sea experiencing the relaxation that comes with an ocean voyage. For others the attraction lies in visiting new places and waking up in new countries while onlyhaving to pack and unpack once, or, as a P&O booklet of the 1950s put it, 'There she lies, your kind, commodious home – the best hotel.'

It could be argued that the first shore excursion was the overland trek between Alexandria on the Mediterranean coast of Egypt and the Red Sea port of Suez for onwards travel to India. Before the Suez Canal was opened in 1869, this faced all travellers to the east, unless willing to undertake the longer sea voyage around Africa. The overland route and way-stations were originally set up by Lieutenant Thomas Waghorn to speed up the journey of army personnel to India, cutting the journey-time by two months. P&O's use of steamships made the journey that much speedier still. *The Hampshire Advertiser & Salisbury Guardian*, 29 August 1840, 'From Alexandria, passengers are conveyed to Afté on the Nile, by track boats, on the canal of Alexandria – a distance of forty-five miles. At Afté a steamer is stationed on the Nile by which the passengers proceed to Cairo – a distance of about eighty miles. The time occupied in this part of the journey varies according to the state of the Nile, but is generally performed in from ten to twenty hours. From Cairo to Suez and vice versa, a distance of seventy-four miles, the journey is performed in carriages, donkey chairs, on camels or on horseback according to the choice of the traveller. The time usually required for passing between Cairo and Suez, including

a reasonable time for repose at the station houses on the road, where beds, refreshments, etc. will be found, is from sixteen to twenty-four hours.' P&O soon began to build up their own network of river boats and hotels. By the mid-1850s, a railway was built between Alexandria and Cairo, later extended as far as Suez, cutting the whole transit time down to just over thirteen hours. The journey still proved arduous for some so in 1868 P&O started sending a purser and a couple of stewards to accompany and assist women and children with baggage until they embarked on the Red Sea steamer. Once the Suez Canal was open this service ceased.

Even in the 1930s, a considerable number of passengers still used the overland route but this time travelling from Port Said to Suez by 'luxurious motor car' in two to three hours. This gave them time to go sight-seeing in Cairo while the ship transited the Canal. One unexpected result of the improvements to travel in Egypt was the rise of tourists to the country. These became so numerous that P&O opened their own hotel in the city.

On the early line voyages to the Mediterranean, time in port was often limited to the loading and off-loading of cargo and mail so passengers might explore local sights or pick up some souvenirs in the bazaar. However, from 1840, passengers wishing to spend longer exploring places such as Vigo, Oporto, Sintra, Cadiz and Seville, had the option of leaving their ship and re-joining it at Gibraltar.

The ships usually anchored offshore. While the port agent would come for the mail, local boatmen would earn extra cash

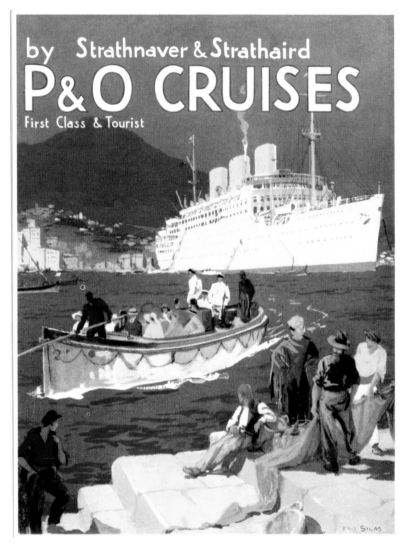

Poster advertising cruises on *Strathnaver* and *Strathaird*, 1930s. © P&O Heritage Collection, reproduced by Kind Permission of P&O Heritage Collection.

ferrying passengers ashore. 'In order to prevent our being cheated by the boatmen, the stewards issued boat tickets at 1s each to go ashore', wrote F. Kendall from Gibraltar in 1859. In some ports such as Funchal, Alexandria and later Port Said, the ships were immediately surrounded by bumboatman selling all kinds of wares – Turkish Delight, trinkets, baskets, hats and so on. The gulli-gulli man was usually allowed on board and would entertain the children (and some adults) with magic tricks. Diana Borcherds, 'I was a Hostess aboard *Chusan* (1950-73) in 1960. During a stay at Port Said a gulli-gulli man was seated after his show having a drink with me, the captain and staff captain. One of the main features of his show was using day-old chicks. The captains were in mess kit and I had on a cocktail dress with a fairly low neckline. We were busy talking when he suddenly called out "Quick Diana, you are smothering my chickens" and everyone turned to me and stared. His sleight of hand was amazing as I was desperately trying to pull out from my low cut dress, chick after chick and they were tweeting madly and scratching my chest. It was one of my most embarrassing moments!'

Arcadia (1954-79) was one of the first P&O liners to have a full summer cruising programme when not operating line voyages. A year after her launch, with a substantial number of anchor ports in the programme, four of the standard lifeboats were replaced by powerful diesel tenders, or 'limousines' as they were called by the crew. Michael Miles was an assistant purser at this time. He recalls that the master, Commodore Forrest, wanted the pursers to learn how to handle these craft as in an emergency he wanted his deck officers at their stations. Michael says, 'Having achieved my degree of proficiency in handling the lifeboat, I took Sir Robert Menzies (then prime minister of Australia) ashore in Malta from where he flew to London for the Prime Ministers' Conference.'

Excursions in the late 1950s offered a selection of half or full day tours, but always getting passengers back on board in time for afternoon tea. Often the ship did not sail until 6 a.m. the following morning, so after tea, a rest and perhaps dinner on the ship, passengers could wander ashore again and see something of the nightlife of the ports. There were still usually more sea days than port days, sometimes as few as three ports on a fourteen-day cruise.

Providing interesting itineraries brings its own challenges. One popular itinerary is to Greenland, Iceland and Norway. These northern waters are not covered by the modern electronic charts used by the vessels, so officers go back to using traditional paper charts. The weather too, can provide its own excitement. Off Greenland in 2011, *Aurora* encountered wind speeds of up to 63 knots with exceptionally high seas. The Log given to passengers at the end of the voyage records that, 'Dense advection fog was encountered during the small hours of the morning and intermittently throughout the rest of the day, requiring increased manning on the bridge as a precaution.' All part of the excitement and adventure in cruising to out-of-the way parts of the world.

Nowadays excursions on offer can vary from a coach tour round a city to white-water rafting or helicopter flights over glaciers in Alaska. Maps and guides accompany presentations on board, so that guests can make the most of their time in port. Marion Weldon has worked for P&O Cruises for seventeen years. She explained her role as tour manager on *Adonia*. As well as organising passengers onto coaches and off on their excursions, she is often able to look around ports and any new attractions that may have opened. If she thinks passengers may enjoy them, she will recommend them to Carnival House for a future programme. The Tour Office is also able to work with individuals or groups to arrange private bespoke tours. Particular challenges may present if the ship is unable to call at a particular port. Given a day or two's notice they may be able to arrange an alternative port by liaising with the agent ashore.

In 2008, a new series of 'Once in a Lifetime' experiences were added to the programme. These offered the chance to drive a Ferrari through the Italian countryside, have a private viewing of St Mark's Basilica in Venice or a flamenco dance lesson in Cadiz. Activities also included guided ice-hiking, cycling and walking.

Top: A stop at a rest house on the overland route between Cairo and Suez in the mid-nineteenth century. © P&O Heritage Collection, reproduced by Kind Permission of P&O Heritage Collection.

Right: Shore excursion brochures of the 1950s. On the *Arcadia* Mediterranean cruise there were just three ports in thirteen days. On the twenty-one night Baltic and southern Norway cruise, there were eight ports, four of which were overnight two-day visits. Reproduced by Kind Permission of P&OSNCo. (*Sharon Poole collection*)

Left: Passengers tendering ashore from *Canberra*, at anchor in the Norwegian Fjords, July 1992. (*Andrew Sassoli-Walker*)

Below: Italian tour buses ready to take *Ventura's* passengers on their excursions. (*Barry Simmons*)

This page, clockwise from top left: Marion Weldon, tour manager on *Adonia*, August 2011. (*Andrew Sassoli-Walker*)

The Shore Excursions desk on *Arcadia*, 2011. (*Andrew Sassoli-Walker*)

Ventura's passengers are tendered ashore at Guernsey, 2008. St Peter Port is a popular destination on shorter cruises. (*Gail Oswald*)

Crew line the foredeck as *Arcadia* reaches Alaska on a seventy-two night round trip voyage from Southampton, 2011. (P&O Cruises)

Oriana transiting the Suez Canal. (P&O Cruises)

Left: Arcadia with *Discovery* moored astern at Alesund, Norway, 2010. *Discovery* is the ex-P&O *Island Princess.* (*Karen Matthews*)

Right: Aurora, on her maiden call at the Canadian city of Quebec, 2004. On the evening she sailed, hundreds of people lined the quayside and city walks to wave farewell. (*Sharon Poole*)

Above: Not every cruise heads for warm waters. On *Artemis'* Christmas Markets cruise in December 2010, passengers were met with deep snow in every port as well as falling on deck. (*Sharon Poole*)

Right: *Oceana* anchored in Palau, Sardinia, with passengers being tendered ashore. (P&O Cruises)

In 2011, passengers on the World Cruises were able to enjoy a new selection of tours to local charity projects. These are designed to support the communities visited whilst offering passengers a unique experience. The first Green World Tours included a children's home in Port Kelang and the Sunshine Village in Phuket. The tours are non-profit making and while some include a donation in the cost, others leave passengers free to donate however much they choose. It is an excellent way of publicising the work of these charities since people often discuss the places visited on their return home.

Left: *Aurora* leaving Istanbul with the famous Blue Mosque in the foreground. (P&O Cruises)

Above: A Breton folk group entertain passengers on *Oceana*, Brest, 21 April 2007. (*Sharon Poole*)

Azura passes St Mark's Square, Venice. (P&O Cruises)

Adonia at the new cruise berth in the Croatian port of Zadar, August 2011. She is reflected in *Greeting to the Sun,* an installation consisting of three hundred solar-powered glass panels set at the same level as the paving. At night it produces spectacular light displays. Close by, and by the same architect designer, Nikola Bašic, is *Sea Organ,* a series of underwater tubes that produce musical chords as waves flow through. (*Caryll Young*)

Glittering West End-style show on *Azura*. (P&O Cruises)

Chapter 11

ENTERTAINMENT & ACTIVITIES

In the early days passengers had to make their own entertainment. At sea they promenaded on deck, read or wrote journals. In the evenings they would gather in the saloon and tell stories, play cards or chess and, for an hour or so, listen to a concert performed by the band. By 1859, a primitive version of deck quoits was being played with rings of hemp thrown into buckets. Another deck game was throwing discs of canvas onto an angled board with numbered and lettered squares, the aim being to hit the winning numbers. In an effort to keep boredom at bay passengers would run sweepstakes on virtually anything – the distance travelled each day was a popular one, but another was what time the ship would tie up at the next port.

By the end of the nineteenth century, as the ships grew larger, with more space devoted to passengers, more amenities could be provided and activities take place. However, being thrown together with other people not of one's choosing could cause the occasional tension. One anonymous writer to the *Himalaya Observer* (daily programme) in 1896 was clearly being sarcastic, 'To the editor: Sir, permit me to express my unqualified appreciation of the great honour conferred upon me by those ladies who so very gracefully recline in my deck chair almost continuously. Although I purchased the chair for my own personal comfort, I am more than repaid by the sense of having innocently done the dear girls an act of kindness. Bless their hearts they shall use my chair if they like – even if I have to stand ...' Steamer chairs could provide their own source of entertainment as Michael Whittingham remembered from a cruise on *Canberra* in 1979, 'Endless amusement

could be had from watching passengers work out how to erect the steamer chairs. There were even instructions in the daily programme, courtesy of an anonymous passenger who penned the following verse:

For those passengers who are unaware,
Of how to assemble a P&O chair,
First lie the chair flat on the deck
The right way up, be sure to check
Now grasp the arms and pull nice and slow,
It will fall into place in just one go.'

On the first day at sea the passengers usually met to elect a sports committee and a chairman, who were then responsible for organising the various tournaments and competitions for the cruise. This system operated well into the early 1960s. As well as card games, chess and charades, daily news sheets advertised dances, music recitals and theatrical entertainment. There was one fancy dress ball per voyage. This usually involved the ship being raided for hats, flags, uniforms, coloured paper – anything that could be turned into a costume! On deck, egg and spoon races, tug-of-war and skipping contests took place, even cricket matches! By the 1930s, these games had been replaced by more adult pursuits such as deck tennis, quoits, swimming and sunbathing.

By the late 1950s there was dancing, film shows twice a week and bingo (or housie-housie as it was then called). If your tastes ran to

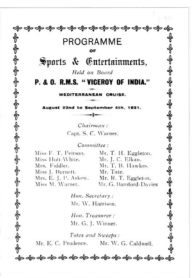

RULES FOR DECK GAMES.

1. Entries for Deck Games, Event 2 [a, b, c and d] will close on Monday, Aug. 24th, at 7 p.m.

2. All games will be played in accordance with ship's rules posted on the notice board.

3. All matches must be completed by the dates specified on the board.

4. All partners in competitions will be drawn for.

5. The first named players will be responsible for arranging their matches. Winners must enter up the results.

6. Semi-finals and finals will be umpired, and umpires will be arranged for by the sub-committee for that particular event.

7. No person will be allowed to compete in any event unless subscription has been paid.

8. In case of dispute, the decision of the sub-committee will be final.

9. Competitors will be allotted numbers, to be worn to assist in identification.

PROGRAMME
OF
Sports & Entertainments,
Held on Board
P. & O. R.M.S. "VICEROY OF INDIA."
MEDITERRANEAN CRUISE.
August 22nd to September 4th, 1931.

Chairman:
Capt. S. C. Warner.

Committee:

Miss F. T. Peirson.	Mr. T. H. Eggleton.
Miss Holt-White.	Mr. J. C. Elkan.
Mrs. Fiddler.	Mr. T. B. Hawkes.
Miss J. Burnett.	Mr. Tate.
Mrs. E. J. P. Askew.	Mr. R. T. Eggleton.
Miss M. Warner.	Mr. G. Bamford-Davies

Hon. Secretary:
Mr. W. Harrison.

Hon. Treasurer:
Mr. G. J. Winner.

Totes and Sweeps:
Mr. E. C. Prudence.   Mr. W. G. Caldwell.

Above and below: Entertainment programme for *Viceroy of India*, 1931. (J&C McCutcheon collection)

PROGRAMME OF EVENTS.

1. **DECK GAMES:** From Aug. 22nd to Sept. 2nd.

(A) **Deck Tennis:**   Ladies' Singles   Men's Singles
Mixed Doubles

(B) **Deck Quoits:**   Ladies' Singles   Men's Singles
Men's Doubles   Mixed Doubles

(C) **Bucket Quoits:**   Ladies' Singles   Men's Singles

(D) **Bull Board:**   Ladies' Singles   Men's Singles

Children's Singles (up to 13 years) for all above Events

2. **Bridge Tournament** (From Aug. 24th to Sept. 2nd)

3. **Treasure Hunt :** Aug. 24th, at 9 p.m.

4. **Dog Races :** Sept. 1st, 2·15 p.m.

5. **Fancy Dress Ball :** *Tuesday, 1st Sept.*

6. **Gymkhana :** Sept. 3rd, from 2·15 p.m.

7. **Prize Distribution and Gala Dance :** Sept. 3rd

PRIZES.

Prizes will be given to winners and runners-up in Event 1 (a, b, c and d), Events 2, 3 and 7, and at the Fancy Dress Ball for :—

(a) Best Costume Made on Board (ladies and gentlemen).

(b) Best Costume Brought on Board (ladies and gentlemen).

(c) Best Fancy Costume.

NOTICE BOARD.

Notices of Competitions, etc., will be found on the board at the after end of " A " deck, and all passengers are asked to watch this board for announcements. Will competitors wear their number cards and assist by arranging to play off heats.

SUBSCRIPTIONS.

LADIES : 5/-   GENTLEMEN : 10/-

Entries for all Events except the Dog Races are free

Passengers are however invited to subscribe to the various gratuities and prize fund.

For the convenience of passengers arrangements have been made to collect subscriptions through their Wine Accounts.

Chits have been circulated for this purpose.

Kindly fill in amount and hand the Chit to your Table Steward.

---

something more active, there was the pool, deck tennis, shuffleboard or quoits. A set of daily programmes from a cruise on *Chusan* in 1959 provides a startling contrast with those of today. On sea days entertainment included aquatic sports, a tea dance, 'horse racing' and dancing to the ship's orchestra. There was a light buffet luncheon served on the Dance Deck and descriptions of what might be seen along the coast. Three films were shown over the fourteen days and bingo or tombola on a couple of evenings. On port days everyone was expected to be ashore, as not only was there no entertainment but no buffet luncheon either. However, since the ship was in port until late evening or early the following morning, local entertainers were brought on board, such as Sicilian Folk Dancers at Messina.

With the move towards more cruising and fewer line voyages there was a corresponding change in the type of passenger and lifestyle on board. They were travelling because they chose to, not because they had to. The atmosphere became less formal and more fun. The old passengers' Sports Committees with their amateur dramatics, recitals and egg and spoon races were replaced in the late 1960s by professional entertainment officers under a cruise director and daily programmes of non-stop entertainment, from keep-fit classes to flower arranging, lectures to films. Michael Whittingham again, 'The highlight of the cruise [on *Canberra*] was Island Night, held round the Bonito Pool. A temporary stage was set up for the band and wires stretched across the pool. Passengers were given streamers to throw over these wires and everyone joined in the singing and waving of flags. It ended with a midnight deck buffet.' There was still a Crew Show well into the 1970s. Peter Bennett was an engineer on *Himalaya* and *Arcadia* around that time. He said, 'The officers were very much involved in passenger entertainment in those days including crossing-the-line ceremonies and sporting activities such as cricket; all great fun and we made life-long friends amongst the passengers many of whom became repeat cruisers (P&O were proud of the record of sixty per cent passenger repeat clients).'

Nowadays, the ships are large enough to cater for many different tastes and varieties of entertainment, from the traditional, such as dancing and deck games – to the cultural, like lectures and recitals – to the spectacular, such as West End style shows. P&O Cruises are one of the few cruise lines to have its own Headliners Theatre Company, set up in 2008. There are seven independent production teams, each one assigned to a specific ship for a six-month period. They perform up to nine different shows on all of the ships. Work will begin on a

Above left: The sports deck and swimming pool on *Corfu* (1931-61). (*J&C McCutcheon collection*)

Aove right: Page from a P&O brochure of 1960, illustrating some of the activities available on board at that time. Reproduced by Kind Permission of P&OSNCo. (*Michael Whittingham collection*)

new show on land, where producers, writers, set designers and makers, choreographers and costumiers will work together to come up with new and exciting shows. On board it will then be up to the cast, band and production crew to turn it into forty-five minutes of sparkling entertainment for passengers. Up to three different shows will be performed, twice or even three times (on the largest ships) in one night in a typical fortnight's cruise.

Cruise Director Neil Oliver, has served on many P&O Cruises ships and gave an insight into his role. He is in charge of all entertainment on board the ship on which he is serving at the time, including headline acts, the production company, after-dinner speakers, dance teachers and lecturers.

Neil has spent over twenty years at sea and, during that time, has met many famous people on the various ships, among them Princess Anne, Larry Adler, Petula Clarke, Helen Mirren, Shirley Bassey, Brian Conley, Sebastian Coe, Jayne Asher, Toyah Wilcox, Jenny Bond and Sue Holderness to name a few.

He described his day, 'There are two types of average day for me. If it is a day at sea I try and dedicate as much time as possible around the ship to visit the various activities and chat to passengers. I am usually in the office early to check any messages and email and of course have a conference with the rest of the entertainment team. The evenings are usually taken up with hosting the various shows and visiting each of our entertainment venues. Port days are a great opportunity to take care of office work, future cruise planning and to read any new policies or procedures. This is also a good time to contact our Southampton office to discuss any other issues.'

Having such a wealth of experience has led Neil to some amusing encounters, but one stood out most for him! 'On the maiden cruise of *Azura* the singer and presenter Claire Sweeney was on board and

P. & O. LINES
s.s. ARCADIA

Official Race Card

THE ATLANTIC OCEAN
Horse Race Meeting

Friday, 11th August, 1967
9.15 p.m.

THE ALBATROSS GLIDE

Mother's Ruin	Mrs Phoebe-Martin	
by Gin out of Bottle		
Black Eye I	Miss Clark	
Wrong Cabin out of Mistake		
Short Pants	Mrs Van Herrewege	
by Runner out of Breath		
No more presents	Mrs Keenan	
by Voyagers out of Money		
Mary Rose	Mrs Ellis	
by Easy Stages out of Bed		
Sun Tan	Mrs Phillips	
by Chemist out of Bottle		

THE LIGHTHOUSE BLINK

White Horse	Mlle F Rossignon
by Whisky out of Bond	
Paleface	Miss Keenan
Keeping out of Sunshine	
No Name	Miss Pemberton
Owner out of Inspiration	
Miss Understood	Owner
Rich Uncle out of Will	
Redskin	Mrs Dear
Blushing out of Modesty	
Scottish Runner	Mrs Gordon
Farrier out of Haggis	

THE PORPOISE GAMBOLE

Tight Again	Mrs Hulme-Vickerstaff
Gin out of Bottle	
Seasick	Mrs Hudson
Storm out of Season	
No Headache	Mrs Phoebe-Martin
Aspirin out of Bottle	
Black Eye II	
Shaking out of Turn	
Windermere	Mrs Light
Moonlight out of Fells	
In the Pink	Mrs White
Showing out of Clothing	

Race 4 — THE BAGGAGE ROOM PILE UP

1 Mr Taylor	Arcadia	
	by Brown's out of Clyde	
2 Mr Kay	Hooray	Mrs Kay
	by First Time out of England	
3 Mrs Woolman	Peepers	Miss Woolman
	by Toes out of Shoes	
4 Mr Kitchen	Round of Drinks	Mrs Tyrer
	by Scotsman out of His Mind	
5 Mr Van Herrewege	Long Pants	Miss Van Herrewege
	by Ribbon out of Place	
6 Mr Ebeling	Fragrance	Mrs Willington
	by Onion out of Salad	

Race 5 — THE STEWARDS' STAMPEDE

1 Mr Moseley	Conquest	Mrs Jasper
	by Wolf out of Darkness	
2 Mr Rawson	Run	Miss Clark
	by Ladder out of Nylon	
3 Mr Van Herrewege	Bare Back	Mrs Scott
	by Lovely out of Pool	
4 Mr Brown	Drink Up	
	by Winnings out of Tombola	
5 Mr Field	White Rabbit	Mrs Field
	by Magician out of Hat	
6 Mr Aykroyd	Lamb Chops	Mrs Aykroyd
	by Butcher out of Carcase	

Race 6 — THE ALDIS SHUTTER

1 Mr Jackson	Hazy View	Mrs Jackson
	by Binoculars out of Focus	
2 Miss Woolman	Mischief	Mrs Woolman
	by 21 out of Control	
3 Mrs Davey	Have you Heard	Miss Davey
	by Rumour out of Ironing Room	
4 Pentargan Co	Can't See	Mrs Soult
	by Focals out of Reach	
5 Mrs Pritchard	Mink	Mrs Cornish
	by Minx out of Sugar Daddy	
6 Mr White	Rolling Home	Mrs White
	by the Light (out) of the Silvery Moon	

Left: Horse racing card, *Arcadia*, 1967.
Reproduced by Kind Permission of P&OSNCo.
(*Michael Whittingham collection*)

Right: Horse racing on board *Canberra*. Passengers turn the wheels to reel-in the 'horses' while passengers bet on which would be the first one home. (*Elaine Brady*)

thankfully (as it turned out) I have known her for many years. During her cabaret, with no prior knowledge and without rehearsal, she called me onto the stage to dance with her. Everything was going great during a very fast salsa and Claire was spinning next to me. The next minute my elbow caught her face resulting in Claire receiving a huge black eye which lasted well over a week. Claire was very understanding about the whole thing and took great delight telling everyone that the cruise director had given her a black eye!'

Of course, entertainment at sea can have its challenges, especially during rough weather conditions! Neil explained, 'If the weather is bad and the ship is moving more than expected, it has been known for us either to alter a performance or to swap it to another night. For example we had a show which contained acrobatics and we decided to programme this to the following night and present a comedian instead.' All just part of the job of cruise director.

A deck party around the Bonito Pool on *Canberra*, from a 1980 brochure. Reproduced by Kind Permission of P&OSNCo. (*Sharon Poole collection*)

Cruise director Neil Oliver on the bridge of *Azura*, 2011. (*Andrew Sassoli-Walker*)

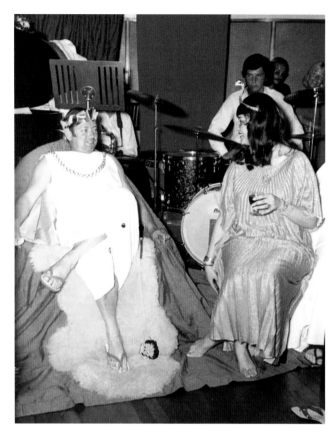

Clockwise from top left: In the days before the ships carried professional entertainment teams, the officers and crew usually put on a performance during the voyage. On *Arcadia* (1954-79) one of Staff Captain Peter Love's favourite party pieces was reciting comic poems, although here he is playing Caesar with Rosie Bull as Cleopatra. (*Wendy Cavaghan*)

Ship's officers formed the *Arcadia* Wurzels, to entertain passengers, 1972. (*Peter Bennett*)

The greasy pole competition on *Canberra*, 1990. Pillowcases were filled with balloons and contestants had to try and knock their opponent into the water. Adults played as well including, on one memorable occasion, Commodore Ian Gibb and Lord Sterling! (*Mark Engelbretson*)

Left: Cruising 1980's style from a P&O Cruises brochure. Reproduced by Kind Permission of P&OSNCo. (*Mark Thomas collection*)

Below: Workmen still finishing painting the shuffleboard courts prior to the maiden voyage of *Ventura*, 11 April 2008. (*Sharon Poole*)

Above: Shuffleboard is still as popular today as it was in times past. (P&O Cruises)

Opposite page, clockwise from left: Playing basketball aboard *Ventura*. (P&O Cruises)

Cooking class led by Marco Pierre White on *Ventura*. *Ventura* was the first ship in the P&O Cruises fleet to introduce celebrity chef Marco Pierre White with his signature restaurant The White Room. His restaurants have since been introduced across the fleet. (P&O Cruises)

The library on *Ventura*. *(P&O Cruises)*

Above left: Jigsaw puzzles are a traditional pastime still popular on all the ships. (*Andrew Sassoli-Walker*)

Above right: A sailaway party on *Arcadia*. (*Barry Simmons*)

Left: A sailaway party on *Oceana* with *Oriana* berthed next to her at St Maarten in the Caribbean, 2006. (*Tim Newman*)

Below: Part of the Gymnasium on *Ventura*. (*Sharon Poole*)

Chapter 12

UPSTAIRS, DOWNSTAIRS

In the early days of steam there was a degree of conflict between the bridge and the engine room. The bridge and navigational team would have trained in the days of sail and there was some resentment at much of the control of the ship being at the mercy of the engineering department. Until the 1880s, steamships were still fitted with masts and a full set of auxiliary sails, not only to be able to increase speed by the use of both engine and sail, but in case of the frequent engine failures of the time. Engine power of the early ships was not very great and many a time when gales hit the Bay of Biscay, a ship would be at full steam ahead, yet effectively remain stationary for hours on end.

From the beginning, P&O normally recruited its captains from the Royal Navy or East India Company, the master being known as commander rather than captain. It was their discipline and knowledge that gave the company its solid reputation for reliability and safety. 'Everything on board is done in regular man o' war style. The ropes are all coiled as neatly as possible, the yards well-squared and the bells sounded punctually every half-hour ... We have just had a test of the state of discipline aboard, the alarm bell suddenly sounding long and loud ... It was merely to place the men at their fire and boat stations and put them through their exercises ...' wrote F. Kendall in 1859. P&O were also unusual in that the ships' officers were kept on board between voyages, instead of the more usual practice of the time of paying off all hands and re-engaging a new crew for each voyage. This encouraged high-calibre officers to remain with the company.

At that time, the command centre was literally a bridge – a narrow walkway from paddle-box to paddle-box with the ship's wheel in the centre – hence the origin of the name. By 1913, P&O offered their own system of cadetships, paying half the fees of those selected, as well as the subsequent apprenticeship premiums. At any time in an officer's career, up to the age of thirty, P&O allowed them to join the Royal Naval Reserve. Those who opted for this had to spend one year serving in the navy, although the time was counted as service to P&O. In those days, P&O engineers were invariably from Scotland, having served their apprenticeships in the Clyde shipyards. By the beginning of the twentieth century, however, they were recruiting from the company's London workshops, with preference given to sons of existing or retired engineering crew who wished to serve apprenticeships.

It takes a lot of people to run a modern cruise ship. On P&O Cruises ships there are between 300 and 1,300 crew, depending on the size of the vessel. The bridge is the hub of any ship, packed full of electronic and computerised equipment, monitoring speed, direction, weather condition, trim, water and fuel tank levels, everything required to operate a large cruise ship with nearly 5,000 people on board. Some things do not change though – there is always a lookout and a person on the helm, even though on board computers could in theory take the ship from A to B without human intervention. There may be no more than half a dozen people on the bridge. The captain and deputy captain are

Officers on *Mongolia* (1923-50). *(J&C McCutcheon collection)*

always there when the ship is entering or leaving port, or navigating through busy or narrow shipping lanes. Otherwise, the officers and crew work to a four hours on, eight hours off system of watches. Every sea day, the captain meets with the heads of all the departments to discuss any issues, problems, forthcoming events and so on. Additionally, each rank of officer has specific duties assigned to them.

Above left: Captain Paul Brown and the second officer on the bridge of *Azura*. The modern bridge is a far cry from the crowded wheelhouses with wooden wheel and engine telegraphs of old, but still has the traditional flag locker. (*Sharon Poole*)

Above right: Richard Bourne, Deputy Captain (once called the staff captain or chief officer), on duty on the bridge of *Ventura*. (*Andrew Sassoli-Walker*)

Right: Crew drills are a frequent and important safety element. Here, *Ventura's* tenders, lifeboats and the safety boat are all in use at Flaam, Norway, 2008. (*Gail Oswald*)

Commodore (of the Fleet)

This post is mainly symbolic and ceremonial and is awarded to the senior captain in the fleet. He has overall pastoral responsibility for the other captains, as well as to the company. In P&O Cruises, at the time of writing, the honour rests with Commodore Steve Burgoine. The ship of which he is master flies the special commodore's flag. This is the same as the P&O house flag, but has a triangular cut-out on the red section. There have been many commodores in P&O's history. Michael Miles recalls Geoffrey Forrest, commodore and master of *Arcadia* (1954-1979). Michael commented that, 'He was ever mindful of the welfare of his crew. When cruising, where the ship had to anchor off, Commodore Forrest arranged for a pontoon to be towed to a nearby beach and for lifeboats to ferry the crew to this pontoon so those off duty could go swimming ... waiters could finish off after breakfast, go to the beach for a swim and return in time to serve lunch.'

Below left: The P&O Cruises' commodore's flag with the triangular cut-out in the red quarter, flying from the jack-staff of *Adonia* as she passes *Ventura* at Southampton, 20 May 2011. (*Andrew Sassoli-Walker*)

Below right: Commodore of the Fleet, Steve Burgoine, on the bridge of *Adonia*, July 2011. (*Andrew Sassoli-Walker*)

Captain

The master of the vessel has overall responsibility for the ship and all on board. As well as being expert in ship-handling, the captain needs to be able to manage the crew as well as being sociable. In 1839, a P&O captain was paid £20 per month – a good wage, since the next highest paid was the chief engineer at £12 per month. The Company Rules in the late nineteenth century were detailed and strict. Captains were not allowed to be seen on passenger decks before 4.30 p.m. and had to be off them by 9.30 p.m. Drinking with passengers was forbidden, as was dancing. Great tact was required at dinner, as long-standing tensions could be caused by perceived snubs as to whom sat next to the captain. Whatever their personality, certain captains attracted their own following, even one particular character in the nineteenth century whose discipline was such that even passengers were lined up outside his cabin at 11 a.m. as defaulters for being late to meals or some other minor infringement!

Nowadays the captain has similar responsibilities. Captain Hamish Reid, master of *Oriana*, now retired, spoke of his years with P&O and P&O Cruises and how things had changed over the period. 'I started working for P&O in 1972. At that time we had over 350 ships in the wider P&O Group, including thirteen passenger ships. They were not known as cruise ships until the 1980s and in particular, the screening of the *Love Boat* television series. The major change has been that they are now designed to take people on holiday and not from one place to another. They are also a great deal more comfortable, more manoeuvrable and customer and crew friendly. When I started only the very expensive cabins had bathrooms in them. Most people had to go down the corridor to toilets and bathrooms/showers.' He said there were too many wonderful ports from which to choose one favourite, although he missed being able to take the large ships into the smaller places that featured in earlier itineraries. Captain Reid hosted a dinner table on most cruises. Two memories that stood out in his years in command were that, 'On one occasion a lady stood up and sang to her husband on their wedding anniversary. It has been etched in my memory ever since! On another occasion I had a couple who had an enormous family dispute which silenced the whole restaurant!'

Not every aspect of a captain's job is pleasant and they may occasionally be required to deal with disruptive passengers. Captain Reid again, 'I have never had to confine a passenger, but I have had some removed from the ship for bad behaviour.'

Captain Hamish Reid with the plaque from the original *Oriana* (1960-86) (see picture on page 172) situated in the captain's meeting room on the current *Oriana*. (*Sharon Poole*)

Deputy Captain

The deputy captain was recently known as the staff captain and in the past as first or chief officer. He is jointly responsible with the captain for the safe navigation of the ship and together with the captain, is always on the bridge when entering or leaving port or navigating narrow or difficult passages. He also oversees the Deck Department, including maintenance, safety and training of crew. Tony Dear recalls a couple of amusing incidents revolving around the chief officer on *Arcadia* (1954-79) in 1964, 'We were doing our turnaround at Southampton. Some of the officers went on leave and when I returned to *Arcadia* I found our newly appointed chief officer was Peter Love and the fourth engineer was Brian Darling. So as we headed down Southampton Water to Australia we had Dear, Love and Darling gracing the good ship *Arcadia*. I was in charge of wheelhouse communications whilst Peter followed the pilot, often out on the wing of the bridge from where, before the days of radios, orders were shouted – orders such as "Head line away, Dear" to which I would reply "Head line away, Love" much to the amusement of the pilots. Another time we were departing the wharf in San Francisco when this gleaming 30,000-ton liner was moving astern, belching forth black smoke from the funnel – "Making smoke below, Dear" to which, of course, the order was repeated "Making smoke below, Love". I picked up the engine room telephone to Brian, "Darling, you're making smoke". The pilot – perhaps with little humour – almost had a seizure, swung the vessel around in record breaking time and vanished, it seemed, from the bridge leaving the master in command!'

First Officer

This officer is usually responsible for navigation. In the early days of the company, this involved checking the chronometers, sextant, compasses and charts. He was also responsible for cargoes – both loading and discharging.

Today, there is no cargo carried but stores still need careful stowage with regard to the trim of the vessel. Although satellite navigation was available from the 1960s, it was almost exclusively used by the US Military. Passenger ships still relied on a sextant – the scientific instrument used to calculate the angle of the sun or stars and the horizon and therefore the position of the ship – well into the 1980s. *Oriana* (1960-86) was one of the very few commercial ships to have a satellite navigation system. Captain Ian Walters recalled that this was

the size of a large American-style fridge and only gave updates every forty minutes! Today, over twenty-four Global Positioning Satellites provide constantly updated information of the ship's position within 10 metres.

Radar is also now linked to the electronic charts, so the very latest information is always available, even when the area is subject to shifting sand bars or new coral reefs. This frees up the time of officers on the bridge to focus on the safety of the vessel.

Second Officer

This is a modern role, in as much as the role of deputy captain was originally called the first or chief officer, as in the Royal Navy. Therefore, in the past it was the second officer who had the navigating duties described above. The second officer in the fleet today is a senior watch keeper and must hold a Chief Mates unlimited license. Duties include maintaining the watch at sea and in port. Other duties include chart and publication maintenance, monitoring the ship's certification, official log book keeping, ballast reporting, davit inspections and assisting the first officer with voyage planning.

Third Officer

In the early to mid-nineteenth century all the mail was accompanied by a Royal Navy officer. However, by the 1870s, it had become the responsibility of the third officer. He was the man faced with all the complicated form filling at every port where mail was offloaded and more delivered to the ship. In addition, he had watch-keeping duties, as well as studying for his mates' certificate if he wished to progress up the ranks. Nowadays, the third officer is a junior watch keeper and holds an Officer of the Watch (OOW) license. They also have a variety of duties such as calculating sunrise and sunsets, assisting the first officer with passage planning, boat inspections and mooring line inspections. The third officer is legally allowed to take charge of the ship with his/her OOW ticket, although this is not permitted by P&O Cruises.

Chief Engineer

In the same way that the captain was always on the bridge when entering or leaving harbour, so the chief engineer was expected to be at his station whenever the ship was likely to be stopped, started or manoeuvred. Today, he heads up the department responsible for all machinery on board from the main engines to the coffee machines. David Jewkes joined P&O in 1971 as an engineer cadet, 'The chief engineer is also a member of the senior management team. My job can be challenging at times as I am always on call, but I enjoy finding solutions to any problems that may arise. We cannot call in a repairman while we are in the middle of the ocean.'

Engine room staff, *Oriana* 1976. (*Peter Bennett*)

Back row, left to right: ? , Geoff Heap (4th Engineer), Mark Sawyer (Jnr Electrical Officer), ? , Paul Robinson (2nd Electrical Officer), John Bates (3rd Engineer).

Fourth row, left to right: Dave Coleman (Jnr Engineer), Dave Scammell (Jnr Engineer), Pat Gallagher (Jnr Engineer), Marty Elliot (3rd Engineer, ?.

Third row, left to right: ? , ? , Malcolm Orr (Jnr Electrical Officer), Steve Musson (Jnr Electrical Officer), ? , ? , ? .

Second row, left to right: Dave Jewkes, (4th Engineer Officer), Trevor Baff (Jnr Electrical Officer), Barry Dover (Jnr Engineer Officer).

Front row, left to right: John Minter (4th Engineer Officer), ? , ? , Peter Bennett (4th Engineer), Ron Dunsford (1st Electricial Officer), Brian Love (Snr Second Engineer), ? , John Bates (3rd Engineer).

Staff Electro-Technical Officer

Originally a radio officer would be responsible for all communications and any electronic equipment. Modern communication systems have made that post redundant as airwave monitoring is automatic. However, the Electro-Technical department is responsible for all computerised systems, from navigation and communication to the in-cabin interactive systems and cyber-studies. P&O Cruises pioneered the development of an Electro-Technical department – the first one on any cruise ship being created for *Royal Princess* in 1984.

Environmental Officer

This is a comparatively recent post – easily recognised on board by the green strip between the gold bands. The officer needs to have a wide knowledge of current environmental legislation and is responsible for making sure the ship complies with various international and maritime laws regarding waste.

Jerry Raynor holds this post on *Azura*. 'On a daily basis, around twenty cubic metres of general burnable waste is processed through the waste disposal area. Our aim is to reduce and recycle as much waste as possible. The department has six crew members, four on day shifts and two on a night shift. Within the day team is a supervisor, responsible for overseeing all operations and maintenance of the equipment. The other five crewmen sort the waste according to how it will be treated – glass, plastic, aluminium, scrap metal, cooking oil, batteries, fluorescent tubes and sludge oil from the engines. All combustible waste goes into the ship's incinerators. Glass and metal is crushed and compacted and landed ashore to a licensed waste contractor. Food waste is pulped and discharged at sea, when well away from land.' Jerry recalled one passenger who thought all the waste was held on board and landed in Southampton as she said she had seen

Top: Engineering officers on *Oriana*, 1976. (*Peter Bennett*)
Back row, left to right: Peter Bennett (4th Engineer), Brendon O'Donahough (4th Engineer), Mike Jack (Jnr Engineer), Dave Scammell (Jnr Engineer), Geoff Heap, (4th Engineer), Conrad Volkner (2nd Ventilation Officer), Martyn Elliot (3rd Engineer), Glyn Dodson (4th Engineer).
Middle row seated , left to right: ?, ?, ?, Douggie Beverage (Jnr Engineer Officer), ?, Dave Grant (Jnr Engineer Officer).
Front row, left to right: ?, Bob Stewart (First Engineer), Arthur Bowness (Chief Engineer), Mike Ramsey (Snr Second Engineer), ?, ? .

Bottom: David Jewkes, Chief Engineer on *Arcadia*, in her main engine room. (P&O Cruises)

trucks moving large bags from the ship. It turned out she had seen luggage being offloaded into the baggage hall!

The environmental officer is also responsible for monitoring the quality of the water. Many passengers wonder at how the ship produces sufficient fresh water for everyone on board. Most of it is made on the ship itself, using de-salination plants. In these, seawater is heated in a partial vacuum by waste heat from the engines and it boils at 85C. It is then condensed into pure distilled water and passes through a chlorination and mineralistion process. It is next tested and stored in tanks for twenty-four hours before being tested again and then piped to the taps. Tanks are used in rotation so that water has time to settle and be retested. The evaporators are most efficient when the seawater is warm and when the ship is running at a good speed. At speeds lower than sixteen knots, there is not enough waste heat from the engines to produce the required amounts. Water is still consumed when the ship is in port so it may be necessary to purchase additional supplies from the port authority if the quality is good enough (a Water Quality Certificate is obtained from each port). If not, the boilers must be used to provide extra heat for the evaporators, but this is used as a last resort because of the fuel cost.

The evaporators can produce 1,000 tonnes of water a day while consumption varies between 600 tonnes and 1,000 tonnes

'Technical water' is made from the same water as the drinking water but it is not further filtered, chlorinated or mineralised. It is used in the hoses and to flush the toilets.

Left: As much waste as possible is recycled on the P&O Cruises fleet. (*Andrew Sassoli-Walker*)

Above: Jerry Raynor, environmental officer on *Azura*. Before joining P&O Cruises he spent many years as a submariner in the Royal Navy. (*Andrew Sassoli-Walker*)

Medical Department

From the earliest days of passenger liners, it was a requirement to have a surgeon on board, although their qualifications were somewhat variable and equipment very basic, especially in the nineteenth century. In *The Standard* newspaper of 28 July 1840, as part of an announcement of a forthcoming new service by P&O to India, it read that, 'Each vessel will carry a Medical Officer appointed or approved of by Government, and the time occupied in the passage home will be allowed in the quarantine.' The main reason for carrying a doctor was to be able to clear the ship of (or treat passengers for) any fever. Homeward bound ships had to spend several days in the Quarantine Harbour at Malta before proceeding, allowing time for any fever caught in Egypt to manifest itself. In 1840, a description in *The Hampshire Advertiser* of the new *Oriental*, mentions 'seven iron beds for invalids, hung on centre so as to swing with the movement of the ship.'

On today's ships, the Medical Department is exceptionally well-equipped. All are accredited by CHKS Healthcare Accreditation Standards and submitted to annual external audits to maintain the accreditation.

The senior doctor on *Azura*, Dr Andre Mostert, gave an insight into his department. As well as himself, there is one other doctor on board so, while Doctor Mostert deals mainly with passengers, the other doctor will run the crew clinics. There is a senior nurse, with three other nurses under their supervision. The ship's Medical Centre is equipped with five beds as well as three intensive care or high-dependency beds, along with laboratory and X-ray facilities and can cope with nearly all emergencies. There are clinics every day and at all times there is a doctor on call; twenty-four hours a day, every day. This duty is shared between them, as is any shore leave. As well as medical matters, the senior doctor also attends the Executive Committee meetings, Public Health rounds, crew rounds and weekly drills.

Every passenger's nightmare is probably that of having to be taken ashore due to a medical emergency but the decision is not one taken lightly. Dr Mostert explained that he had to deal with a medevac (helicopter airlift from ship to shore) a few months ago, 'It saved the passenger's life. We will usually do it for surgical emergencies. It is not without risk though and weather, distance from the shore, shore-side facilities and the general condition of the patient will be considered before a decision is made by the doctor, captain and shore-side medical director.' Two of Dr Mostert's most memorable patients were not even sailing on board the ship. 'We picked up two fishermen south of the

The Quarantine Harbour, Malta, 1870. Homeward bound ships had to spend several days here before proceeding, to allow time for any fever caught in Egypt to manifest itself.

Dominican Republic after their fishing boat developed mechanical problems. They were drifting at sea for a week before we came to their rescue, spotting them purely by chance. They had to catch fish and drink their blood to survive. Needless to say they needed urgent medical attention at the time but both survived the ordeal.'

Incidentally, it was following an emergency medical transfer from a cargo ship to the *Arcadia* (1954-79) in the Indian Ocean, that the limitations of having to use lifeboats for this purpose were apparent and requests were made for the ships to carry small, fast sea-rescue craft, launched from a single wire fall, instead of the twin fore and aft falls on normal lifeboats. These are now standard on every cruise ship.

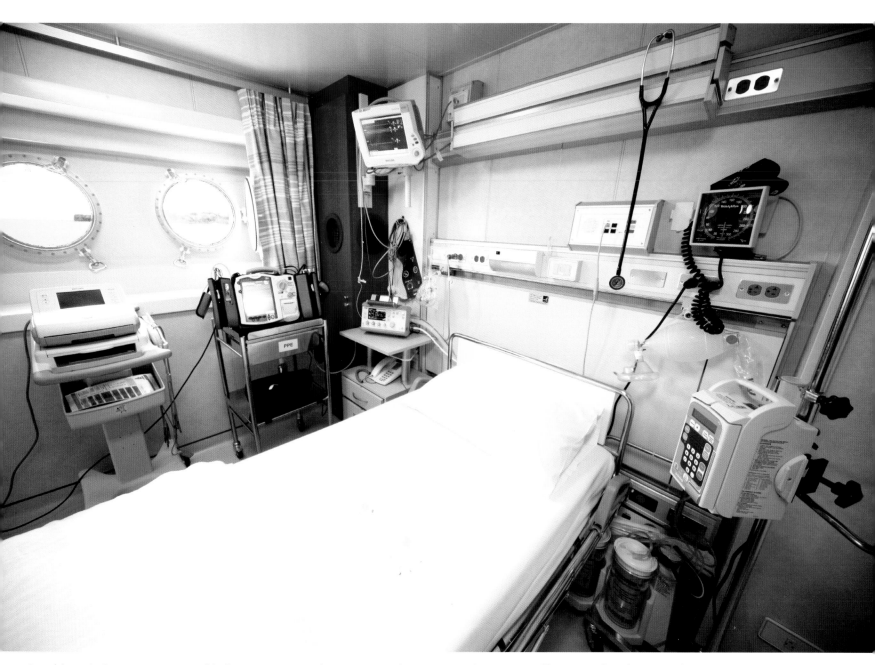

Part of the medical centre on *Azura*, one of the few areas on a cruise ship passengers are happy not to see, but are reassured knowing it is there. (*P&O Cruises*)

This page: On 23 November 1965, there was an emergency on *Canberra* when a ten-week-old baby was diagnosed with pneumonia whilst halfway between Honolulu and Auckland. A Royal New Zealand Air Force Sunderland was despatched with oxygen cylinders which were dropped into the sea close to the ship during the morning. Later that evening they rendezvoused with a US Coast Guard cutter, *Cape Providence*, which rushed the baby to Samoa for urgent medical treatment. (*Patrick Sutcliffe*)

Executive Purser & Hotel operations

The hotel side of a ship is run separately from the operation of the ship herself. Up to the 1870s, the purser had sole responsibility for this department. He had charge of victualing for both passengers and crew, as well as furnishing the vessel with everything from beds to napkins, towels to teacups. He managed all the stewards and was financially responsible for the entire inventory of the ship, although he had powers to withhold a percentage of the stewards' wages to cover loss or damage to items. The nature of the job brought him into daily contact with passengers and diplomacy along with tact and discretion was a requirement of the job, although the occasional 'disciplining' of passengers could also be necessary, especially in the cramped and enclosed conditions of the early ships. The Company Handbook of 1860 pointed out that, 'From the moment the passengers come aboard until they leave the ship they are particularly under your care, and your attention to their comfort on board must therefore be unceasing.'

By the mid-twentieth century, with the huge increase in the size of ship and number of passengers carried, the purser's department had grown ten-fold.

Nowadays in the largest ships in the P&O Cruises fleet, such as *Ventura* and *Azura*, the housekeeping department consists of 193 crew, eighty-seven cabin stewards, sixty assistants, twenty-eight laundry staff, eight officer stewards, three butlers, six deck housekeepers and one florist, each playing their part to help the ship run smoothly.

Above: Bureau staff, *Canberra*, December 1965. (*Patrick Sutcliffe*)
Back row, left to right: John Simmonds, Dave Baumann, Paul Batt, Patrick Sutcliffe, Paul White, Geoff Smith, Roy Michelson.
Front row, left to right: Maureen Price, Liz Twine, Marian Rodenburg, Nell Reinsma, Liz Hall, Gill Cuffley.

Below: The Bureau with its staff of pursers, *Canberra*, 1965. (*Patrick Sutcliffe*)

From Bell Boy to Executive Housekeeper

In 2012, Stephen Radford will have served thirty-eight years with P&O, Princess and P&O Cruises and has seen many changes over the years. In fact, going to sea was quite the opposite of what Stephen wanted to do, which was to be an air steward. His interest in air travel came from a very early age, when he travelled with his parents every year to Malta. So keen was he on this ambition, he was the first ever boy at his school to study Domestic Science. Although this proved to be a very difficult time for Stephen, it did not diminish his resolve and he passed. He planned to take a Catering & Hospitality course at Henley College, but while waiting to become old enough to apply, his father spotted an advert in a newspaper for hotel staff with P&O, which would give him valuable experience in the meantime.

Once accepted, his first job was as tourist-class lift bell boy on board *Canberra*. It was not long before he was promoted to first-class bell boy. Stephen's attention to detail shone through, to the degree of finding out which cabins passengers on the captain's table occupied and being ready and waiting for them with the lift when they finished dinner. He shared a story that the first-class passengers tipped very well, allowing him to buy his parents their first colour television as a gift when he came home on leave. When it was delivered it took some time for him to explain that he wasn't involved in anything illegal!

Left: Stephen Radford, executive housekeeper, *Adonia*, August 2011. (*Andrew Sassoli-Walker*)

Above: Stephen Radford, second-class lift bellboy, *Canberra*, c. 1971. (*Stephen Radford*)

He was soon promoted to assistant cabin steward and it was not long before he was promoted again to cabin steward when his senior had to leave suddenly. He was young to hold the post and once again, had a hard time from some of his colleagues. However, with support and advice from two older stewards, he put to rest any doubts as to his abilities.

When *Canberra* was requisitioned for the Falklands Conflict Stephen was on leave. He tried to phone the company to ask to re-join his ship, but his mother disconnected it before he got through!

When *Royal Princess* entered service in 1984, he was asked to transfer but didn't care for the way Princess Cruises' stewards worked in pairs and that, together with his love for *Canberra*, put him off – until the third time of asking. As Stephen's parents got older however, he returned to P&O to be closer to home (*Royal Princess* was based in Los Angeles). In a twist of fate, in 2005, Stephen was reunited with *Royal Princess*, when she joined P&O Cruises as *Artemis*, where he worked as accommodation manager up to her leaving the fleet in 2011. He is currently housekeeping manager on *Adonia* and funnily enough has no regrets about not taking to the skies.

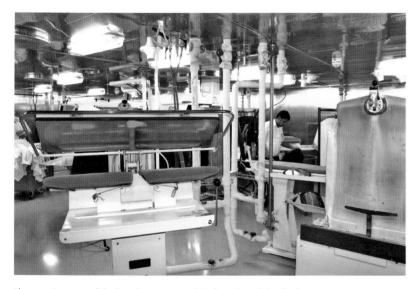

The pressing area of the laundry on *Azura*. (*Andrew Sassoli-Walker*)

Christine Bick, deputy housekeeper on *Azura*, in front of one of the industrial washing machines in the large laundry. (*Andrew Sassoli-Walker*)

Uniforms in the laundry, freshly cleaned and pressed ready for delivery to *Azura*'s crew. (*Andrew Sassoli-Walker*)

Christine Bick explained her role as deputy housekeeper on *Azura*, 'The executive housekeeper and the deputy housekeeper oversee the operation, with the executive housekeeper looking after the cabins while the deputy, with the help of an assistant, looks after the public areas, laundry, florist and baggage operations.' Christine had been with P&O Cruises for only ten weeks when she spoke with us, having previously been executive housekeeper for a large hotel group. She felt she needed new challenges, so decided to leave her husband, son and family behind in the UK and set out on a new career at sea. She said, 'It was all so daunting at first, wondering what had I let myself in for, but I wish I had done it years before. The people are wonderful, they have something special about them, they welcome you into their lives; One Big Family is what always springs to mind. In the first few weeks I kept getting lost, but so many of the crew laughed with me and pointed me in the right direction and, even now after ten weeks, they smile when they see me. Life on board a ship is completely different from shore side. There, baggage was something the guests in hotels brought with them; now there is a four-hour operation to bring on thousands of bags, but with team work it all gets done and delivered. My husband is proud of what I have achieved and without his support I could not be where I am today.'

Butlers and Stewards

If any post required discretion it was that of a steward! They built up a rapport with the regular passengers, so much so, that in the past, especially on line voyages, many regular travellers always asked for cabins under their care. Nowadays, the more expensive suites go one step further and passengers have the services of a butler.

Anil, Arun and Girish are three butlers on *Azura*. They described their average day at sea. 'We begin by serving early morning tea or coffee followed by breakfast. We then tidy the suites and top up the fridges with ice, lemon, fruit and drinks as requested. By mid-morning we will be around the ship making bookings for our passengers at the tour desk, spa, or the fine dining restaurants on the ship. We usually make about fifty dining reservations each. Mid-morning is 'Pimm's time' or perhaps a glass of gin and tonic, whatever the guest enjoys, followed by lunch served on the suite balcony – weather permitting. The evening begins around tea-time when we serve canapés and champagne or maybe a nice glass of wine. Formal evenings bring on an added challenge as we get their attire pressed, compliment the ladies on their beautiful gowns and maybe help the gentlemen with a tricky bow-tie! We also arrange cocktail parties in the suites, serving drinks and canapés to the guests ... many times we also double up as the DJ!

Another personal touch we can provide is discussing the dinner menus and perhaps recommending dishes. We can advise on the entertainment for the evening as well as what to look forward to the next day as regards weather and what to do in port.'

Left: Anil, one of the three butlers on *Azura*, prepares champagne for embarking suite passengers. (*Andrew Sassoli-Walker*)

Above: One of the top suites on *Azura*, set up in twin-bed configuration. (*Sharon Poole*)

Below: A deluxe balcony cabin on *Oriana*. (*P&O Cruises*)

Assistant Front of House Manager

Joshua Nixon, assistant front of house manager on *Azura*, explained the role of his department. 'The reception is manned by a team of eleven, of which eight work at the reception desk, one in accommodation, one in the crew office and one at night. They can rotate to each department as and when needed. I report to the front of house manager and am responsible for the rota of the receptionists, disembarkation of over 3,000 passengers, shuttle buses, turn-arounds and general issues with the desk. Before working for P&O Cruises I completed a four-year degree in Hospitality Business Management at Birmingham University. I then worked in the United States for a few years before joining P&O Cruises around eight months ago. Life at sea is very different from life on shore. For a start it's a 24/7 job but it's very enjoyable and the time flies by, as every day is different, especially on Reception.'

Crew on board a cruise ship develop strong bonds as they become part of a team. To this end, they are not above the occasional practical joke, especially on newcomers. Darren Deegan again, 'When I joined, the usual "induction" for new staff (if you were soft enough to fall for it) was to be asked to go on "Fog Watch". This consisted of standing at the front of the ship in your lifejacket looking for fog with a pair of binoculars at night! It was all meant in good fun.' As Darren went on, 'Training of staff who are new to the sea and making them feel comfortable and welcome is part of my job as premier sous chef. The galley team is like a large family so some days you have to be the dad, mother, brother or sister.' A senior engineer also remembered, 'You needed a sense of humour. It doesn't happen nowadays but you never knew what the lads would do to your cabin while you were out. I can remember once they took the hinges off the side of the cabin door and placed them on the top so that it opened up like a garage door!'

The Reception Desk on *Azura*. (Andrew Sassoli-Walker)

Crew

The heads of departments are responsible for hundreds of crew. Before the opening of the Suez Canal, British sailors were employed on the UK–Alexandria sector and Asian crews from Suez onwards. After the opening of the Canal in 1869, the deck crews on board P&O ships were almost exclusively Lascars from Pakistan, while the stewards and waiters were from Goa. 'The crew were all inspected by the Captain this morning; they were nicely dressed in white calico with various-coloured sashes according to their rank or occupation.' So wrote William Anderson while travelling aboard one of his company's ships in the mid-nineteenth century. The Lascars were expert seamen and coped better with the heat of the Indian Ocean. Crews were changed every twelve to eighteen months and as time went on, it became traditional for sons to follow fathers into the service of the company. An office was set up in Bombay (now Mumbai), to employ and train P&O and now P&O Cruises staff.

Shannon May is Crew Manager on *Aurora*. 'On a port day I will be meeting our port agent and any immigration and Customs officials that may board during our arrival with the paperwork they need to clear the ship's crew. If we have crew leaving or joining the ship in that port I will confirm transfer/flight details with the agent and meet the crew as they arrive or before they depart. I also have to make sure all crew are back on board before we sail. On a big turnaround day we can have as many as 240 crew leaving at the end of their contract and the same number joining to start work – this is a very busy day in the Crew Office. We have to make sure each crew member has the right documents to join the ship. A valid medical certificate that shows they are fit for their tour of duty, passport and visas for immigration at each port, customs and next of kin information for our records. If the crewmember works in the Deck or Technical department we have to ensure we have copies of their certificates of competency along with any safety certificates we require such as fire fighting, first aid, crisis management.

We have 842 crewmembers on board, made up of twenty-seven different nationalities (I am one of just four New Zealanders on *Aurora* currently). Crew welfare is very important. Occasionally, crew need to go home early for compassionate or medical reasons. This isn't a nice part of my job but it is rewarding when we can get them home as soon as possible.

I have met some of the best people during my time at sea, including my fiancé Martin, who was the Crew Manager while we were both on *Artemis*. We are getting married in April and I have returned to P&O Cruises because I really enjoy the work.

Right: Lascar deck crew in traditional dress on *Viceroy of India* (1929-42). (National Maritime Museum, Greenwich)

Far right: Crew manager, Shannon May and assistant manager, Ian Fuller in *Aurora's* Crew Office. (*Andrew Sassoli-Walker*)

Passengers

The story of a cruise ship cannot be complete without the passengers, since without them, there would be no P&O Cruises. From the earliest days of P&O Steam Navigation Company, when the main purpose of the ships was to carry mail, passengers were always treated with care and consideration – something that has continued ever since. Michael Miles recalls that when the concert pianist Benno Moiseiwitsch travelled on *Arcadia* (1954-79) to Australia in the 1950s, 'a piano was specially muted so that he could practise daily without disturbing other passengers. Not every passenger reciprocated unfortunately.'

Children are catered for equally as well as adults and have been for many years. Mark Engelbretson's contemporary account as a child on *Canberra*, 'The thing I like best about *Canberra* is the freedom you get because you hardly see your parents at all ... their programme is never ending even when in port, they cater for all likes and a child never seems to be bored at any time during a cruise.'

Nowadays there is a complete Youth Crew, known as the Reef Rangers. These may number up to fifty on the larger ships in the summer holidays, all devoted to entertaining children and teenagers from morning till night. The children's facilities are called The Reef and activities are organised for four age ranges – two to four-year olds, five to eight, nine to twelve and thirteen to seventeen. There is also a night nursery for babies to five-years olds, so parents can enjoy dinner and a show or the casino.

Richie Iles is youth programme manager at Carnival House. His main priority is putting the young passenger first, 'A child's development and safety is paramount in everything I consider. We operate all day, every day and aim to cater for every child, whether creative, artistic, one that loves games or computers. All of our child care is included in the fare, from the night nursery for little ones, to the children's tea to the sports coaching. Simple things like using one of our buggies, bottle warmers or cots make it easier to travel, especially if flying out to join one of our ships. We try and think of everything when it comes to families.'

Zoe Dance is youth director on *Oceana*. She describes a typical day for her. 'My mornings consist of getting activities ready for the day, arranging any extra equipment or venues if required, ordering special meals for children with food allergies, ordering birthday cakes and updating staff of any changes. I check the sports nets to ensure that the football coach has everything he needs – water for the children, bibs and equipment. I will then look into all the clubs making sure

Above: The first-class nursery on *Strathmore* (1935-63). Reproduced by Kind Permission of P&O Heritage Collection & P&OSNCo. (*Sharon Poole collection*)

Left: The tourist-class nursery on *Himalaya* (1949-74). Reproduced by Kind Permission of P&O Heritage Collection & P&OSNCo. (*Sharon Poole collection*)

Singer Clara Butt, her husband Kennerly Rumford and children, embark *Mongolia* at Tilbury bound for Australia, 1907. (*J&C McCutcheon collection*)

everyone is enjoying themselves. After lunch I will go to the club swim.
I will host a children's party for the next hour, with party dances, prizes
and lots of fun. Then it will time for children's tea in The Plaza where
I will chat to families or, on a couple of nights of the cruise, Noddy
or Mr Bump will come to tea with the children – these occasions are
always very popular. Tea is usually followed by a magic show. There
are many highlights of my job but seeing the children leave with the
biggest smile on their faces and hearing them tell their parents about
all the fun and exciting things they have been doing all day has to be
the best reward.'

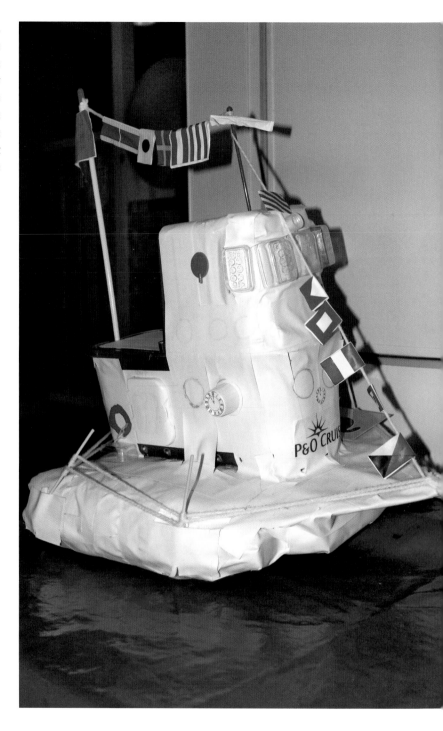

Right: Model of *Azura*, made by children during one of their activity sessions. (*Andrew Sassoli-Walker*)

Opposite page, clockwise from left: Up-to-date video-gaming technology keeps children entertained. (*Andrew Sassoli-Walker*)

Children are well catered for with extensive toys and activities on board. This is The Beach Hut on *Azura*, for two- to four-year-olds. (*Andrew Sassoli-Walker*)

Above: Teenagers can chill out with new-found friends in *Azura's* Apartment 16. (*Andrew Sassoli-Walker*)

Right: Noddy welcomes children to *Ventura*. (*Sharon Poole*)

Below: The Reef children's area on *Ventura*. (*Sharon Poole*)

Chapter 13

2012 & BEYOND

An event as significant as celebrating the tracing of P&O Cruises roots back 175 years to that first mail contract, awarded to The Peninsular Steam Navigation Company in 1837, could not go unmarked, and the P&O Cruises celebrations have been in the planning stages for many months. The main event will be the gathering together of all seven ships in Southampton on 3 July 2012. This will be the first time in P&O Cruises history that the whole fleet has been in its home port at the same time. The ships will process down Southampton Water before sailing their separate ways on a variety of cruises varying in length from four to twenty-one nights, to four points of the compass – north to the Baltic and Norway, west to Ireland, east to the Netherlands and south to the Mediterranean and Atlantic Islands.

As the excitement of this Grand Event worked its way through to passengers and all those involved in P&O Cruises, there was more to come with the announcement of a new ship to join the magnificent seven in 2015. This vessel will be the largest P&O Cruises ship built to date at 141,000grt and, as Micky Arison, CEO of Carnival Corporation, commented, 'Underscores our commitment to leading the expansion of this important region'. The design too, is a departure from current vessels and, if current plans come to fruition, will be the first since *Canberra* to have twin funnels, making her instantly recognisable and carrying on the diversity, innovation and tradition that is P&O Cruises.'

P&O cruises Managing Director Carol Marlow continued, 'This next-generation ship will deliver the ultimate P&O Cruises experience, with "sophisticated wows" and new features to attract thousands of newcomers to our brand and equally, to resonate with existing P&O Cruises passengers by giving them the 'P&O-ness' they recognise and love. She will offer the best of the best, combining the favourite classic features of *Oriana* and *Aurora*, the choice and variety of *Azura* and *Ventura*, with a host of new ideas and concepts which together will deliver to our passengers the holiday of a lifetime, every time they travel with us.'

One of the first things that people started to discuss after the new ship was announced was the name. This can often incite controversy as different people have different ideas as to whether a traditional name should be resurrected or a new name invented as in *Ventura* and *Azura*, but whatever her name, she will carry forward the iconic P&O Cruises fleet and take her place in the history books of this great company and, in being Britain's favourite cruise line (as voted four years running by readers of the *Daily Mail* and *Mail on Sunday*), perhaps William Thackeray's famous phrase can be brought up to date – the sun never sets on a P&O Cruises ship!

Artist's impression of the new P&O Cruises' ship due to enter service in 2015. When launched she will be the largest ship in the fleet. (P&O Cruises)

In conclusion

British people have shown an even greater love of cruising in recent years, and they now take over 1.6 million cruises each year. With that number set to grow and P&O Cruises being the favourite British cruise line, we have an opportunity to introduce more and more British people to this great style of holiday. I look forward to the next 175 years of cruising!

Micky Arison

Chairman and Chief Executive Officer, Carnival Corporation and plc

Micky Arison, Chairman and Chief Executive Officer, Carnival Corporation and plc

Watching the wake of a ship can be hypnotic. (*Andrew Sassoli-Walker*)

'On sunny noons upon the deck's smooth face
Linked arm in arm, how pleasant here to pace;
Or, o'er the stern reclining, watch below
The foaming wake far widening as we go.'
Arthur Hugh Clough 1819-1861

BIBLIOGRAPHY & FURTHER READING

Cable, Boyd, *A Hundred Year History of the P&O*, Ivor Nicholson & Watson Ltd, 1937

Canberra – The Great White Whale goes to War, The Peninsular & Oriental Steam Navigation Co., 1982

Dearest Mother, Extracts from the Letters of F. R. Kendall, P&O Cruises, 1987

Howarth, David & Howarth, Stephen, *The Story of P&O*, Weidenfeld & Nicholson, 1986

Ingall, Carola, *The P&O Line and Princess Cruises, A Celebration in Pictures*, Ship Pictorial Publications, 1997

Maxtone-Graham, John, *Liners to the Sun*, Sheridan House, 2000

McCart, Neil, SS *Canberra 1957 – 1997*, Fan Publications, 1998

Mitton, G.E., *Peeps at Great Steamship Lines – The Peninsular & Oriental*, Adam & Charles Black, 1913

P&O in the Falklands, The Peninsular & Oriental Steam Navigation Co., 1982

Padfield, Peter, *Beneath the House Flag of the P&O*, Hutchinson, 1981

Penney, Michael, *Sea Officer*, published by styrman29@yahoo.co.uk

Pugh, Nicci, *White Ship Red Crosses*, Melrose Books, 2010

Quartermaine, Peter & Peter, Bruce, *Cruise, Identity, Design & Culture*, Laurence King Publishing Ltd, 2006

Rabson, Stephen & O'Donoghue, Kevin, *P&O, A Fleet History*, World Ship Society, 1989

Robinson, Anthony, *Rain Stopped Play*, Zeus Publications, 2009

Sassoli-Walker, Andrew & Poole, Sharon, *Artemis, The Original Royal Princess*, Amberley Publishing plc, 2010

Sproule, Anna, *Port Out, Starboard Home*, Blandford Press Ltd, 1978

Thackeray, William Makepeace, *From Cornhill to Grand Cairo*, 1844

Wall, Robert, *Ocean Liners*, Collins, 1978

Williams, David L., *Glory Days of P&O*, Ian Allan Publishing Ltd, 1998